COZY
Stitches

COZY Stitches

12 Calm & Creative Embroidery Projects
for Absolute Beginners & Beyond

CELESTE JOHNSTON
Lemon Made Shop

BETTER DAY BOOKS®
HAPPY · CREATIVE · CURATED

Download all the embroidery patterns
featured in this book at
www.betterdaybooks.com/cozy-stitches-pattern-download

Library of Congress Control Number: 2024931401

ISBN: 978-0-7643-6858-5
Printed in China
10 9 8 7 6 5 4 3 2 1

Copublished by Better Day Books, Inc., and Schiffer Publishing, Ltd.

Better Day Books
P.O. Box 21462
York, PA 17402
Phone: 717-487-5523
Email: hello@betterdaybooks.com
www.betterdaybooks.com
@better_day_books

Schiffer Publishing
4880 Lower Valley Road
Atglen, PA 19310
Phone: 610-593-1777
Fax: 610-593-2002
Email: Info@schifferbooks.com
www.schifferbooks.com

This title is available for promotional or
commercial use, including special editions.
Contact info@schifferbooks.com for more information.

DEDICATION

This book is dedicated to my loving and
supportive husband, Taylor. Thank you for being
the most wonderful dad to our kids and for filling our
home with humor, warmth, love, and care.
Home is wherever I am with you.

Contents

70

78

86

94

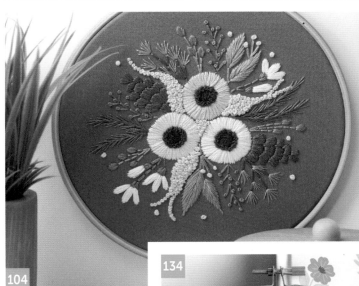

104

114

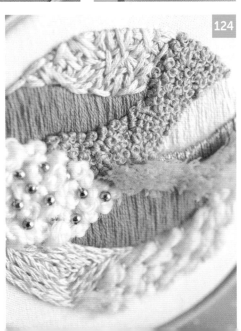

124

134

Stay Awhile

SLOW
DOWN

8

Welcome

Hi there!

I'm thrilled that you're here and ready to cozy up and stitch with me! It has been an amazing experience to have written a third book of my embroidery patterns for absolute beginners, and it means the world to me that you would join me in the fulfilling, creative, and therapeutic hobby of embroidery.

If you're brand new to the world of embroidery, you have so much joy coming your way! I think you'll figure out pretty quickly that embroidery is an absolutely charming and captivating hobby.

If embroidery is already a beloved craft for you, I'm so glad you're here too. I hope you gain a new insight or two, and I'm appreciative that you want to make something today with my patterns!

I have been a crafter all my life, but it wasn't until more recently that I discovered a love for embroidery. I was drawn in at the first stitch as I realized how much it encouraged me to slow down and create something beautiful with my hands. I've learned that the craft has other perks too. The gentle weaving of the needle through the fabric is a restorative, therapeutic process that will keep your hands engaged for hours, leaving you with a feeling of accomplishment. It's also a practical and portable craft with inexpensive supplies and no mess!

My hope and intention when setting out to create the projects for *Cozy Stitches* was to curate a collection of patterns centering on the warmth of home. My inspiration came from cozy sweaters, cool weather, gentle florals, and all the warm and fuzzy feelings of being home with loved ones. If you've picked up this book, I'm hoping these are some of your favorite things too, and I wonder which pattern you'll start stitching first!

With this book, I also hope that when the weather is cold, you might invite a group of friends or family members together to enjoy the revered tradition of embroidery. Bake something comforting and delicious, make hot tea, and provide plenty of embroidery supplies, and you'll have the essentials for an embroidery party!

As you work through the book, please keep in mind that embroidery is an opportunity to express your creativity, and this book is meant to be used as a restorative part of your day. You may even view it as a form of self-care, nurturing the creative side of you and spending time doing something for yourself that you truly love to do. You can follow the patterns and colors just as I created them, or let yourself play with any colors and alterations that you feel drawn to. Your embroidery may not look exactly like mine, and that's okay. Mistakes and do-overs are part of the process, and because embroidery is such a forgiving craft, there's no need to be hard on yourself. You are well on your way to creating adorable works of art for your home or as gifts to loved ones. Take your time, take care of yourself, and enjoy the process!

Love,

Celeste

Meet the Author

What do you love about embroidery?

I love the warmth and texture a piece of embroidery brings to a space. I also love how easy it is to sit down and pick up without mess or preparation. However, it's the process that draws me in. The rhythmic motion of filling in patterns with beautiful colors is very therapeutic. It's a hobby that has been engaging women for hundreds of years, and I love being a part of that heritage.

Where do you live?

My family and I live right outside Austin, Texas, and I am originally from Peoria, Illinois.

Where do you stitch? Do you have a designated studio?

I share a home workspace with my husband, Taylor. I use my desk for sketching, transferring patterns, choosing floss colors, and working on the business side of my art. But I usually stitch on my comfy couch in front of the TV, outside watching my kids play, or in a coffee shop listening to podcasts, audiobooks, or phenomenal playlists that my husband creates for me.

Check out Celeste's other books, *Freshly Stitched* and *Sunny Stitches*!

You have a significant following on Instagram; can you tell us how that platform inspires your work?

I love being a part of the global embroidery community through Instagram. It's incredible to see the variety of art created with the simple medium of needle and thread. My Instagram account started as a way to share with friends, and it grew organically to a community of more than 100,000. I'm pretty introverted and never expected to have such an audience, and now—three books! I think it is enjoyed by so many because I share tutorials and tips for embroidery. I try to be consistent in my style and authentic to myself, sharing highs and lows. I engage with my "Instagram friends" as if they are friends in real life, having conversations about stitching, life, plants, and everything in between.

In addition to being a busy designer, artist, and entrepreneur, you are a mama to two adorable kiddos. How do you balance it all?

Being a mom, artist, author, and entrepreneur is a lot to balance. I have to carefully choose what I commit to, which means getting comfortable saying no when something doesn't fit or bring me joy. I sometimes struggle with meeting the demands of my family and work. Ultimately, I put my family's needs first because I recognize that these years are fleeting. Thankfully, I have a supportive husband who has an equal hand in parenting our kids.

What do you hope readers will get from this book?

I hope they will feel empowered to create something new with the patterns and instructions I have provided. I hope they make a lifelong connection with embroidery. And I hope they gain as much happiness from this fulfilling craft as I have.

Celeste's Cozy Stitching Playlist

"Slow Burn"
BY KACEY MUSGRAVES

"Homesick"
BY KINGS OF CONVENIENCE

"She's Got You"
BY PATSY CLINE

"So Many Plans"
BY BEIRUT

"Bring It on Home to Me"
BY SAM COOKE

"Steadfast"
BY S. CAREY, JOHN RAYMOND & GORDI

"All Too Well [Taylor's Version]"
BY TAYLOR SWIFT

"A Running Start"
BY SUFJAN STEVENS

"Song for Zula"
BY PHOSPHORESCENT

"Cool About It"
BY BOYGENIUS

"Light Years"
BY THE NATIONAL

"The Boxer"
BY SIMON & GARFUNKEL

"Me at the Museum, You in the Wintergardens"
BY TINY RUINS

"Space Song"
BY BEACH HOUSE

"The Trapeze Swinger"
BY IRON & WINE

"River"
BY JONI MITCHELL

"Our Way to Fall"
BY YO LA TENGO

"Pink Moon"
BY NICK DRAKE

Getting Started

If this is your first experience with embroidery, the tutorials in this section will provide all the information you need to get started. Be sure to stitch the sampler project to try out all the stitches and develop your skills. For even more information, check out the appendix on page 143.

Let's start stitching!

Fabric

When you set out to embroider a design, the first element to consider is your background fabric. This is the foundation of your project that will allow your beautiful stitching to shine. Choosing the wrong fabric will result in puckering or stretching, which would be such a disappointment after putting your time and effort into stitching the design. My best advice is to keep it simple—choose a common quilting cotton or linen fabric with no elasticity. To expand on that, here are a few details to keep in mind.

Type

If you're a beginner, I recommend a loose-weave fabric such as muslin or osnaburg. These fabrics will help you practice the basics of stitching because the needle and floss can slide through them so easily. They're inexpensive, come in natural or white colors, and are readily available at any craft or fabric store.

My favorite fabric for beginners and experienced stitchers alike is Kona cotton. If that's not available to you, choose any high-quality quilting cotton, which will have a high thread count, feel very smooth, and suit nearly any embroidery project. I also frequently stitch on linen or linen blend fabrics.

Embroidery on thick or stiff fabrics such as denim or canvas is possible, but these are a bit of a challenge to stitch through. Avoid any fabrics with stretch because they will warp your designs.

Color

Choosing just the right colors for your projects can be such a fun exercise in creativity. When it comes to fabric, I prefer stitching on solid colors, but feel free to get adventurous and choose a fabric with a subtle pattern.

When I stitch on a light color, such as white or peach, I like to double up the fabric to create an opaque background. It's slightly easier to transfer patterns onto light fabrics than dark ones, which is something to keep in mind when choosing your fabric colors.

While transferring the pattern may be more challenging, it's possible to stitch on dark fabrics. For these fabrics, white carbon transfer paper or sticky fabric stabilizer will be your friend!

Preparing Your Fabric

Before you start stitching, there are just a few things you'll need to do to prepare your fabric.

- If your fabric has substantial wrinkles, iron it before transferring your pattern onto it.
- If you're stitching on fabric that will be removed from the hoop once the project is complete (a shirt, for example), preshrink it by washing it before stitching.
- Decide if you want to use one or two layers of the fabric, depending on its thickness and color.
- Use a good pair of fabric scissors to trim your fabric to size. I recommend trimming your fabric into a square with 2 to 3 inches of excess on all sides.

15

Floss

You know you love embroidery when you behave like a kid in a candy store in the thread aisle, adding to your basket each and every color that catches your eye. It's a good thing that embroidery floss (or thread) is inexpensive, because you'll want to have a variety of colors on hand to experiment with different combinations.

Type

Basic cotton embroidery floss is sold in skeins of six strands loosely banded together. For each of the projects in this book, you'll need one skein or less of each color noted in the supplies list. The project instructions also note how many strands of each color you'll use to stitch the different areas of a design. Read about how and why to split your floss in the tutorial on page 24.

In addition to the ever-popular and versatile cotton floss, you'll find specialty flosses such as pearl (perle), satin, metallic, tapestry wool, or silk. These are fun to incorporate into your pieces, and we'll experiment with them in the Starry Night project on page 86 and the Blush Meadow Abstract project on page 124.

There are quite a few different brands of embroidery floss widely available, but for this book, I used DMC floss. The specific color numbers are listed in the Floss Color Index on page 150. Feel free to use any floss brand and colors you prefer.

Storage

There are several ways to store embroidery floss. Some stitchers like to wind their floss on small white bobbins and store them in a thread organizer. Others use clothespins or wooden spools to keep their floss neat and tangle-free.

Beads

Beads and sequins can be stitched onto your fabric to add a little bit of sparkle and shine to your work. Take a walk through the beading aisle at your local craft store to see what catches your attention. You can add beads with just a little bit of technique to add color and sparkle as you please throughout the designs in this book!

TIP: Keep long floss scraps to use for other projects. I keep a little jar at my workspace for these useful leftovers.

Embroidery Tools

One of the many reasons embroidery is a beloved and timeless hobby is because the necessary tools are inexpensive and easily accessible. If you're a crafty person, you probably have most of these essentials in your home already. Here are the tools you'll want on hand in your embroidery basket.

Hoops. Embroidery hoops are made of a metal tightening mechanism and two rings that grasp your fabric and hold it taut, creating the right surface for stitching. You can find embroidery hoops in all sizes, but for this book, you'll need only 4", 5", 6", and 7" hoops. You can purchase hoops at your local craft store. Also keep an eye out for them while shopping at thrift stores.

Scissors. Keep two types of scissors on hand in your embroidery basket: fabric shears and embroidery scissors. The shears are for cutting your fabric to size. The small and very sharp embroidery scissors are for trimming threads, especially in compact spaces.

Needles. For the projects in this book, basic size 5 embroidery needles are perfect, but you may want to try a few different sizes. Purchase a pack of assorted-size embroidery needles so you can experiment. I like to use smaller needles when I'm working with one or two strands of floss only. I have learned that tapestry or crewel needles are necessary when working with yarn or tapestry wool. If you're adding beads to a piece of embroidery, you'll want to find a beading needle or a needle with a shaft and eye narrow enough to fit through the beads.

Needle minder or pincushion. You'll want to have a place to set aside your needle when you need to take a break or change floss colors. Use a magnetic needle minder or a pincushion to keep your needle from getting lost.

Needle threader. This optional tool can be very helpful for threading your needle.

Glue. Fabric-safe glue can be used to finish the back of your embroidery project.

Cardstock. Thick paper like cardstock is useful for finishing the back of an embroidery project.

Transfer pens. There are several types of fabric transfer pens available to you. I like to use a black heat-erasable pen for most projects. Once you finish stitching, you use a hairdryer to erase any visible pen marks. You may also like a blue water-soluble marker, which washes away with water once you're finished stitching. A chalk pencil is handy for transferring patterns onto dark fabrics.

Carbon paper. Tracing patterns onto dark or thick fabrics is difficult. Instead, I use these tissue-thin transfer sheets. You'll find them in the needle arts aisle of your local craft store.

Transferring Your Pattern

Once you've chosen your fabric, you'll need to transfer a pattern onto it. The patterns for the projects in this book start on page 152. Use one of the methods below to transfer a pattern onto your fabric.

Tracing

Use your preferred fabric transfer pen to trace the design onto your fabric. You can tape the pattern to a sunny window, tape the fabric on top, and then trace the design. This method is easy and cost effective!

You can also use a light table or create a makeshift one using your phone's flashlight and a clear tote lid. My preferred method is a makeshift light table with a heat-erasable pen, pictured at the right.

To make the pattern easier to see behind the fabric, especially if your fabric is dark, go over the lines of the pattern with a dark, fine-tipped marker before tracing.

Transfer Paper

Carbon transfer paper works really well when you're using dark or thick fabrics that you can't see through to trace a pattern. To transfer a pattern using carbon paper, layer the pieces together with your fabric on the bottom, then the transfer paper, then the pattern on top.

Use a stylus or ballpoint pen to trace over the pattern. The pressure will transfer the pattern lines onto your fabric. If the transfer is light, use a transfer pen to touch up the lines so you can clearly see where to stitch. This is my preferred method for transferring patterns onto dark fabric.

Fabric Stabilizer

These paper or fabric sheets are also sold at your local craft store. To use this method, you'll transfer the pattern onto the stabilizer, then attach the stabilizer to your hooped fabric following the package instructions provided. You stitch right on top of the stabilizer and then remove the excess when you're finished.

Step by Step: Tracing Your Pattern

STEP 1: **Trim the fabric.** Cut a square of fabric slightly larger than your chosen pattern. I like to leave 2" of extra fabric on all sides of the design. Iron out any wrinkles. Note: If you use two layers of fabric for stitching, you need to transfer your pattern only onto the top layer.

STEP 2: **Choose your light source.** Using tape, secure your pattern over a light source. I like to create a makeshift light table with my phone's flashlight and a tote lid. Center your fabric over the pattern. Choose a tracing pen.

STEP 3: **Trace.** Take your time and trace the pattern carefully. Once you finish, remove your fabric from the light source and make any necessary touch-ups with your transfer pen.

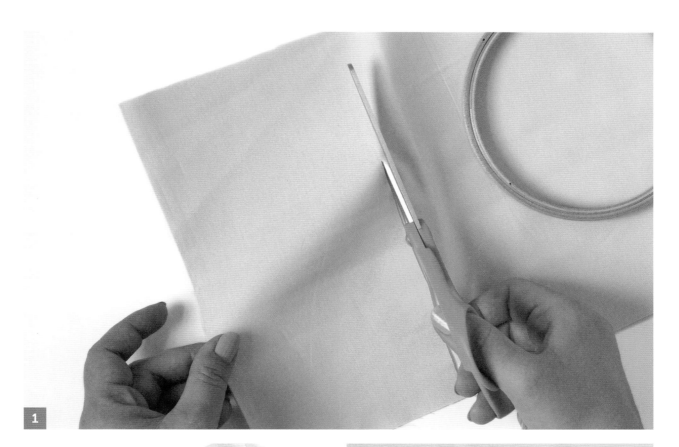

21

Setting Your Hoop

After you've transferred your pattern to the fabric, you'll secure the fabric in an appropriately sized embroidery hoop. Use the size listed at the beginning of the project to choose a wooden or plastic hoop that nicely frames the design. You'll need a clean, flat surface like a desk or table to set your hoop.

Step by Step: Setting Your Hoop

STEP 1: Separate the hoops. Separate the inner and outer hoops by unscrewing the tightening mechanism and pulling the hoops apart.

STEP 2: Position the fabric. Lay your fabric on top of the inner hoop, centering the design over it. Place the outer hoop on top of your fabric.

STEP 3: Put the hoops together. Keeping the design centered neatly in the hoops, press down on the outer hoop. It will expand to fit over the inner hoop, sandwiching the fabric in between.

STEP 4: Secure the hoops. Carefully tighten the screw on the outer hoop to hold the hoops in place.

STEP 5: Pull the fabric tight. Work your way around the hoop, gently pulling the fabric taut around the edges every quarter turn. Be sure to keep the design centered in the hoop.

STEP 6: Check the fabric. Take your time and be sure the fabric is centered, pucker- and wrinkle-free, and taut. Your fabric should be drum-tight, meaning it will sound like a drum when you tap it with your fingers.

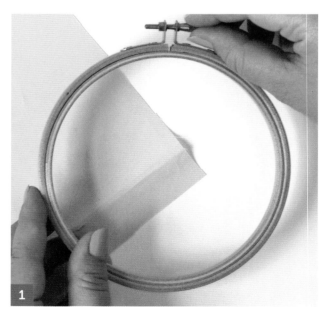

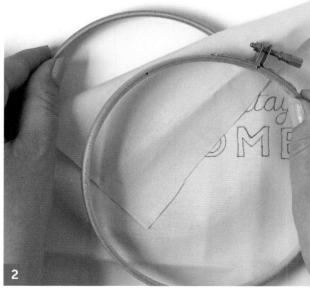

Stitching

Embroidery floss is made up of six strands. You can vary the number of strands you use to stitch your design to create different looks. When you're stitching the projects in this book, the instructions will note the number of strands needed for each element in the design. Now that you've set your hoop, it's time to separate the number of strands you need from your embroidery floss skein, thread your needle, and start stitching.

Step by Step: Separating the Floss

STEP 1: Cut the floss. Cut a length of floss about 12" to 18" long.

STEP 2: Separate the strands. At one end of the floss, use your fingers to separate one strand from the rest.

- -

TIP: Always pull the floss from the numbered end of the skein to avoid a tangle.

STEP 3: Pull. Pull on the single strand with one hand while you hold the rest of the floss in place with the other hand. Once the strand is separated completely, set it aside.

STEP 4: Repeat. Repeat until you have as many strands as you need for your design. Lay them together.

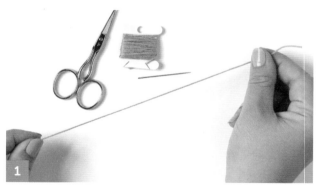

Step by Step: Start Stitching

STEP 1: Thread the needle. Hold your embroidery needle in one hand. In your other hand, hold the very end of the floss strands between your thumb and index finger. It may help to lightly dampen the floss. Press the eye of the needle over the end of the floss and pull a few inches of floss through the needle. (You can also use a needle threader instead.)

STEP 2: Secure the thread. Tie a single knot at the other end of the length of floss, about ¼" from the end.

STEP 3: Bring the needle to the front. Starting with the needle behind the fabric, push it through to the front, pulling the floss with it. The knot you made in step 2 will secure the end of your floss at the back of the fabric.

STEP 4: Practice stitching. Now you're ready to stitch away! Try a few up-and-down straight stitches to get the feel of embroidery. Make the Cozy Quilt sampler on page 32 to practice your stitches.

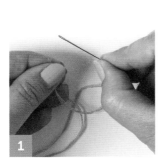
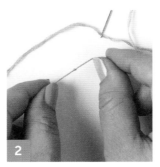
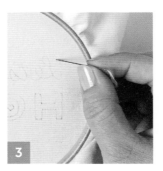
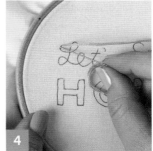

Step by Step: Finish Stitching

STEP 1: Trim the floss. When you've finished stitching, are nearing the end of the floss, or want to switch colors, bring the floss to the back of the fabric and trim it, leaving a 2" tail.

STEP 2: Tie the floss. Split the strands of floss into two evenly sized bundles and tightly tie them into a knot against the fabric.

STEP 3: Finish. Trim the floss tails to about ¼" long.

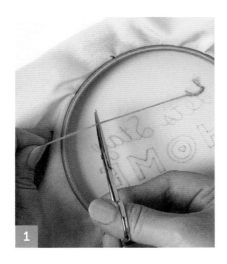
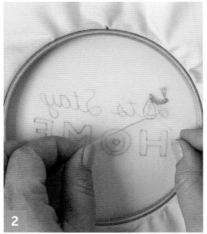

Finishing the Back of Your Hoop

After you've completed a piece of embroidery, it's time to finish it so you can display it. Traditionally, the back of a hoop is stitched closed with a running stitch. This pulls together all the excess fabric, gathering it at the back. Then this is covered with a circle of felt stitched to the excess fabric. Alternatively, you can use the quick gluing method outlined on the next page with a fabric-safe glue. Either way, before you finish the back of your hoop, there are a few final steps to complete.

Finishing Touches

- Ensure your stitching is completely finished—if you use glue to close the back of the hoop, you won't be able to make edits to the piece later.

- Trim any excess floss tails on the back.

- Remove any remaining transfer pen marks according to your pen's packaging instructions.

- Gently tighten the fabric and check the tension of the hoop's screw.

Step by Step: Finishing the Back

STEP 1: Cut the circle. Take an embroidery hoop that's the same size as your finished project and trace the inner hoop on cardstock. Cut out the circle.

STEP 2: Trim the fabric. Trim the excess fabric at the back of the hoop, leaving about 1" around the edges.

STEP 3: Add the circle. Place the cardstock circle in the hoop against the back of your stitches.

STEP 4: Glue. Add a thin ring of fabric-safe glue around the edge of the cardstock circle and the back of the inner hoop.

STEP 5: Secure the fabric. Fold the fabric over the edge of the inner hoop and firmly press it in place on the cardstock until it sticks.

STEP 6: Repeat as needed. If you stitched your design on multiple layers of fabric, repeat steps 4 and 5 with the second layer of fabric.

Now your hoop is ready to be displayed! Use a small finishing nail, pushpin, or even a bit of twine and colorful washi tape to hang your hoop on the wall. Your finished piece could also rest on a mantle or bookshelf.

- -

TIP: Before adding the circle to the back of your hoop, sign and date it, or, if you're gifting the piece, inscribe a message for the hoop's recipient on it.

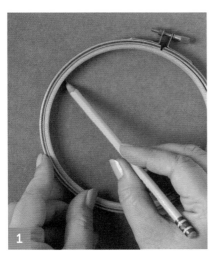

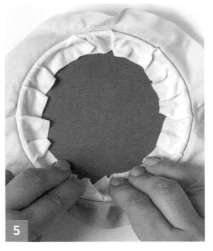

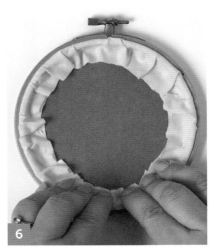

Wear It or Share It

Once you get comfortable with embroidery, I think you'll have a lot of fun thinking outside the hoop and dreaming up projects to wear or share. You can add embroidery to clothing, accessories, and pieces of home décor like linen napkins, decorative banners, or pillows, among many other keepsakes and textiles.

Adding embroidery to your clothing by stitching directly on it or by creating a wearable patch can make such a cool and personal statement. Use any of the patterns in this book, or combine small elements from them, to create just the right design for your garment.

When stitching on a garment like a hat, shirt, or baby blanket, there are just a few things to keep in mind.

- Wash the fabric to preshrink it so it doesn't warp or distort your stitching when you wash it later.

- Use a stabilizer to reinforce your stitching, especially if you're working on fabric with a little stretch.

- Use a hoop to keep your work surface pulled taut.

- Keep your stitches very short, no longer than ¼", to avoid loose, pulled stitches.

- Once your stitching is complete, handwash your garment as needed to protect the delicate embroidery.

Botanical elements from Mindful Mandala on page 134 and Gentle Notes to Self on page 38 customize these children's garments.

This canvas tote and pouch got a makeover with my Starry Night and Booked All Weekend projects on pages 86 and 114.

Make something just for you! This belt bag is adorned with a leafy branch from the Simple Countryside Bouquet project on page 78. Spruce up a set of cloth napkins with the Winter Botanicals project on page 104. You can see I'm using sticky stabilizer paper to mark the pattern on this brown linen napkin. This type of stabilizer is great for working with dark fabrics and washes away with water.

Notes about Self-Care

Embroidery can be so fun and completely captivating that you may not notice the hours passing by. Here are some tips for keeping your stitch sessions relaxing, enjoyable, and frustration-free.

Lighting

All that time spent carefully concentrating on your work can strain your body and eyes.

Protect your eyes by stitching in bright, natural light (you can even work outdoors in the shade!). If you have to stitch at night, invest in a craft lamp that can be positioned directly over your work. I like to clamp a small book light onto the edge of my hoop. Proper lighting will make quite a difference in the neatness and consistency of your stitches. Even more important, it will help reduce eye strain.

Posture

As you work, take note of your posture. It is ideal to work seated in a supportive chair. Pay attention to signs that your neck, back, or hands need a rest. It may help to set a timer at regular intervals as a reminder to stand up, stretch, and take inventory of your environment. You are important, so please remember to take care of yourself!

Troubleshooting Tips

As you stitch, you'll inevitably encounter pesky knots. Working slowly with short lengths of floss (18" long or less) will help you keep knots to a minimum.

As you pull the floss through the tightly stretched fabric, it will become twisted and strained. Periodically, stop stitching and let your needle hang down from your hoop so the floss can unwind. Then you can start stitching again. If you notice a knot forming as you pull the floss through the fabric, stop as soon as you see it and gently use your needle to pull on the strands and untangle it.

Anytime you encounter a problem while you're stitching, you can always stop, carefully snip the stitches with your embroidery scissors (avoiding the fabric), pull out the floss, and begin again with a new length of floss. Embroidery is a very forgiving craft!

Cozy Quilt Sampler

Are you ready to practice some stitches?
This Cozy Quilt sampler will help you get acquainted
with the 15 embroidery stitches used to create
the projects in this book. Use the pattern on page 35 or 165
and the Embroidery Stitch Library on page 144, settle in,
and get cozy! You can use any fabric and floss colors
that make you happy to create this design.

QUICK REFERENCE

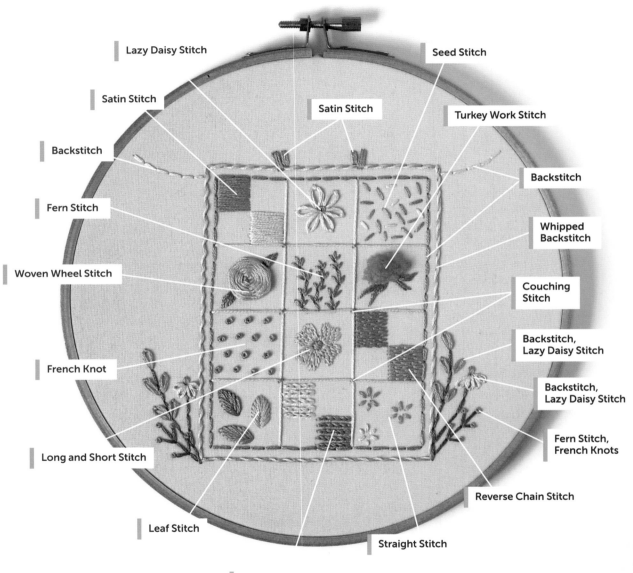

Lazy Daisy Stitch

Satin Stitch

Backstitch

Fern Stitch

Woven Wheel Stitch

French Knot

Long and Short Stitch

Leaf Stitch

Split Backstitch

Satin Stitch

Seed Stitch

Turkey Work Stitch

Backstitch

Whipped Backstitch

Couching Stitch

Backstitch, Lazy Daisy Stitch

Backstitch, Lazy Daisy Stitch

Fern Stitch, French Knots

Reverse Chain Stitch

Straight Stitch

Cozy Quilt sampler pattern
(removable pattern sheet also on page 165)

The Projects

I had so much fun creating the projects in this
book, and I hope you'll have just as much fun
stitching them. As you prepare to stitch a design,
don't forget—embroidery is an opportunity to
express your creativity! Follow the patterns and
colors exactly or let your imagination run wild.
No matter what, have fun!

Gentle Notes to Self

STITCHES

- Backstitch
- Straight stitch

SUPPLIES

- 4" embroidery hoop
- 7" x 7" piece of your chosen fabric
- 1 skein of each floss color: light mocha, light pine green, mustard
- Embroidery scissors
- Embroidery needle
- Transfer materials (page 20)
- Finishing materials (page 26)
- Pattern (page 153)

Slow down. You are enough. Let yourself rest. Take a deep breath, and let's get ready to stitch something together just for you! Choose one of these three simple and gentle notes to self to encourage yourself to find rest daily and to live a life with slow and meaningful purpose. I chose these three mantras because they are what help me pause and enjoy the small, important parts of life. I hope they resonate with you too.

If embroidery is a new hobby to you, you're starting in the right place! These designs use only the most basic embroidery stitches with just a handful of floss colors so that you can concentrate on the message and not have to worry about much else. I used a simple white cotton fabric and chose calming floss colors like light pine green and light mocha. I used mustard floss for the tiny stars, but you can substitute gold metallic cotton floss if you feel like experimenting with something new today. Feel free to use whichever floss and fabric colors draw you in, and enjoy getting started with this stitching project! ■

Leaves and Branches
Light pine green |
Backstitch | 4 strands

Stars
Mustard |
Straight stitch |
1 strand

Pine Branches
Light pine green |
Backstitch | 4 strands

Pine Needles
Light pine green |
Straight stitch |
4 strands

Text
Light mocha |
Backstitch | 4 strands

TIP: A note about knots: As you stitch, you'll inevitably encounter pesky knots. Working slowly with short lengths of floss (18" long or less) will help you keep knots to a minimum. As you pull the floss through the tightly stretched fabric, it will become twisted and strained. Periodically, stop stitching and let your needle hang down from your hoop so the floss can unwind. Then you can start stitching again. If you notice a knot forming as you pull the floss through the fabric, stop as soon as you see it and gently use your needle to pull on the strands and untangle it.

40

STEP 1: Prepare your materials. Following the tutorials in the Getting Started section, transfer your pattern, set your hoop, and separate your floss. Thread your needle with four strands of light-mocha floss.

STEP 2: Start the text outline. Using four strands of light-mocha floss, make a ⅛" stitch along the first letter, ending with the needle behind the fabric. Bring the needle up through the fabric about ⅛" from your first stitch. Stitch backward, pushing your needle through the hole at the end of your first stitch. Your stitches will be touching and sharing the same holes in the fabric. This is called backstitch.

STEP 3: Finish the text outline. Continue outlining all the letters with backstitch. Keep your stitches equal in length as you work. Short stitches make it easier to outline curves than long stitches.

STEP 4: Stitch the pine branches.
Using four strands of light-pine-green floss, backstitch the centerline of each of the two pine branches. Keep your stitches short and uniform, about ⅛" to ¼" long. Then, using the same floss, add a straight stitch to create each pine needle. Start your stitch at the end of the pine needle and end the stitch at the backstitched centerline.

STEP 5: Stitch the leafy branches. Using four strands of light-pine-green floss, backstitch the branches and leaves.

STEP 6: Stitch the stars. Using one strand of mustard floss, straight-stitch over the small star details. Start by stitching one short horizontal straight stitch and then cross over it with another slightly longer straight stitch. Use small straight stitches for the details.

STEP 7: Finish. Follow the steps on page 27 to finish the hoop. Remove any transfer pen marks as needed.

TIP: Once you feel comfortable with the progression of your stitching skills, try adding your own words to the patterns. You can choose any daily affirmation or gentle note to self you like and simply write it on the fabric. Or use a computer to print the text and trace it if you wish.

44

STITCH DIARY

*"Since time is the one immaterial object which
we cannot influence—neither speed up nor slow down, add to
nor diminish—it is an imponderably valuable gift."*
—MAYA ANGELOU

Have you stopped to take care of yourself lately? I know keeping busy and working hard are necessary and unavoidable parts of life. They're often how we fill our time without a second thought. But rest isn't a luxury; it's an important and key part of self-care for our minds, bodies, and spirits. It's essential for us to have rest and downtime and to recognize when we've given enough of ourselves.

**Take a moment to assess how you take care of yourself.
What are your favorite ways to rejuvenate? What's missing?
What are some things that you can do to build in
sustainable pockets of self-care or rest?**

_____

_____

_____

_____

_____

_____

_____

_____

Vanilla Latte

STITCHES

- Whipped backstitch
- Backstitch
- Split backstitch
- Straight stitch
- Fern stitch
- Lazy daisy

SUPPLIES

- 6" embroidery hoop
- 9" x 9" piece of your chosen fabric
- 1 skein of ivory floss
- Embroidery scissors
- Embroidery needle
- Transfer materials (page 20)
- Finishing materials (page 26)
- Pattern (page 154)

To me, nothing is cozier than a warm vanilla latte! Enjoyed at home, in a coffee shop, in a bookstore, or in my car on the go, it's always my favorite pick-me-up. While this embroidered latte won't give you the same boost of energy and warmth found in a cup from your favorite barista, it will look adorable hanging in your kitchen or stitched on a canvas tote, and it might just be a cheerful invitation for you to sit down and take some time for yourself.

This project will introduce you to several more basic stitches that we'll use frequently throughout the book. Take your time learning these new stitches, and don't forget to practice on a separate hooped piece of fabric if it's your first time trying them out. Settle in with your favorite warm beverage and let's get started. ∎

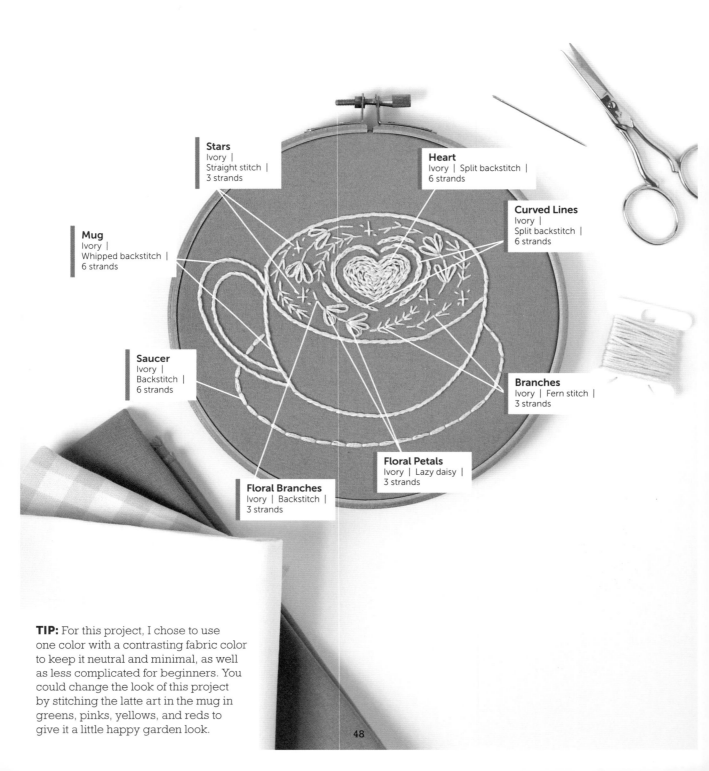

Stars
Ivory |
Straight stitch |
3 strands

Heart
Ivory | Split backstitch |
6 strands

Curved Lines
Ivory |
Split backstitch |
6 strands

Mug
Ivory |
Whipped backstitch |
6 strands

Saucer
Ivory |
Backstitch |
6 strands

Branches
Ivory | Fern stitch |
3 strands

Floral Petals
Ivory | Lazy daisy |
3 strands

Floral Branches
Ivory | Backstitch |
3 strands

TIP: For this project, I chose to use one color with a contrasting fabric color to keep it neutral and minimal, as well as less complicated for beginners. You could change the look of this project by stitching the latte art in the mug in greens, pinks, yellows, and reds to give it a little happy garden look.

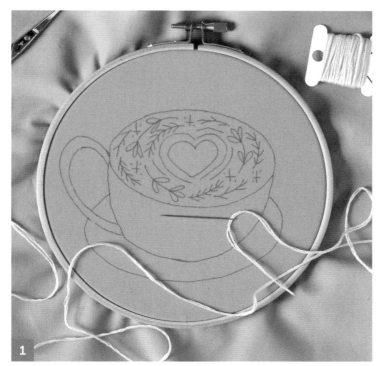

STEP 1: Prepare your materials. Following the tutorials in the Getting Started section, transfer your pattern, set your hoop, and separate your floss. Thread your needle with six strands of ivory floss.

STEP 2: Start outlining the mug. Using six strands of ivory floss, outline the mug with backstitch.

STEP 3: Finish the outlining the mug. Now it's time to complete the whipped backstitch. Using six strands of ivory floss, bring your needle to the front of the fabric at the left corner of the mug. Guide the needle under the thread of the first backstitch. Bring your needle over the first backstitch and guide it under the second backstitch. Repeat, pulling the floss gently as you wrap it around each backstitch you made in step 2. When you reach a corner or the end of a length of outline, bring your needle to the back of the fabric to secure the thread. Continue until you have stitched along the entire outline, then bring your needle to the back of the fabric.

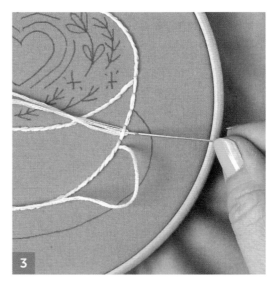

STEP 4: Stitch the saucer. Using six strands of ivory floss, outline the saucer with backstitch.

STEP 5: Stitch the heart. Using six strands of ivory floss, fill in the heart with split backstitch. Starting along the edge of the heart, make a ¼" straight stitch. Bring your needle up about ¼" away from the end of your first stitch. Stitch backward, pushing your needle through the middle of the first stitch, splitting the six strands of floss in half. Continue making split backstitches along the edge of the heart. Then add additional rows of split backstitch to fill in the center. The guidelines will help you keep your rows neat and aligned.

STEP 6: Stitch the curved lines around the heart. Using six strands of ivory floss, stitch the curved lines around the heart with split backstitch.

STEP 7: Stitch the stars. Using three strands of ivory floss, straight-stitch the stars and accent marks.

STEP 8: Stitch the branches. Using three strands of ivory floss, stitch the branches with fern stitch. Start with a row of backstitches for the centerline. Then add short straight stitches where the backstitches meet.

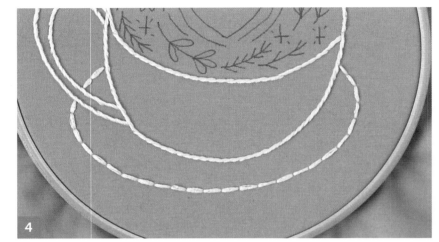

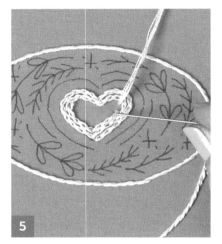

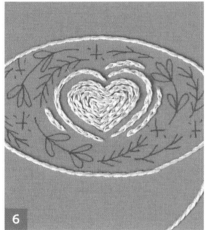

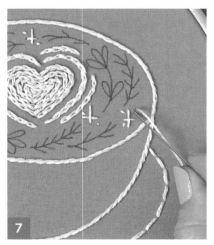

STEP 9: Stitch the floral branches. Using three strands of ivory floss, outline the floral branches with backstitch.

STEP 10: Stitch the floral petals. Using three strands of ivory floss, outline the floral petals with lazy daisy stitches. Start by making a very short stitch, but do not pull the thread all the way through. Instead, let it form a ½" loop on top of the fabric and hold it gently in place. Bring your needle up through the fabric where you want the top of the loop to be and feed it through the loop. Pull the thread tight to bring the loop down against the fabric. Enter the fabric just above where the needle came out, capturing the top of the loop in the stitch. Repeat for each petal.

STEP 11: Finish. Follow the steps on page 27 to finish the hoop. Remove any transfer pen marks as needed.

TIP: Embroidery is a very forgiving craft, and learning from your mistakes and mishaps is part of the process. This is a gentle reminder that your stitches don't have to be perfect or permanent. Anytime you encounter a problem while you're stitching, you can stop, carefully snip the stitches with your embroidery scissors (avoiding the fabric), pull out the floss, and begin again with a new length of floss.

STITCH DIARY

"Thank you, Coffee. For everything.
You make life possible. I don't want to make you feel weird,
but you are my soul mate. Well done."
—JEN HATMAKER

When my son was born 10 years ago, I came to a particular realization
about myself that I think a lot of new parents also acknowledge. Among so many
other things, I learned that I felt peace when I had structure and routine in my life.
I knew that if I woke up first and had a few quiet moments to myself in the kitchen
before everyone else was awake and ready, my day would start out on the right
foot. I would make coffee and mentally prepare for my day. The caffeine helped,
of course, but it was mainly just the moments to be myself. This daily ritual has
come and gone over time, but I love it when I get to start my day
with quiet and coffee because of the peace it brings me.

What routines or daily rituals
nurture peace and calm in your life?

_____

_____

_____

_____

_____

_____

Stay Awhile

STITCHES

- Backstitch
- Lazy daisy
- Straight stitch
- Satin stitch

SUPPLIES

- 3½" x 5½" oval embroidery hoop (or 6" circular hoop)
- 8" x 8" piece of your chosen fabric
- 1 skein of each floss color: maroon, khaki green, white, light brown, dark gray
- Embroidery scissors
- Embroidery needle
- Transfer materials (page 20)
- Finishing materials (page 26)
- Pattern (page 155)

A couple summers ago, my family welcomed a new member, an energetic, affectionate, and fluffy little puppy we named Daisy. She has grown into a large, loyal, and precious part of our lives, and we look forward to many happy years with her. She has imparted me with so many lessons, but one in particular stands out—she has taught me about sitting and resting. Anytime I sit down on the couch, she jumps up next to me and lies down on my lap, where I'm stuck to simply sit and snuggle her. Dogs are really the best, aren't they?

Stitch this project, composed of simple stitches perfect for a beginner, for the dog lover in your life, and take to heart the message: "Stay awhile." All the other work can wait; just sit and enjoy this time of peace and quiet with your favorite craft! Hint: Embroidery is made even better when you have a loving canine companion with you on the couch or at your feet. ■

Pillow
White | Backstitch | 3 strands

Dog Outline
Light brown | Backstitch | 3 strands

Pillow Tassels
White | Straight stitch | 3 strands

Greenery Branches
Khaki green | Backstitch | 3 strands

Greenery Leaves
Khaki green | Lazy daisy | 3 strands

Dog Paws, Nose, and Eyes
Dark gray | Satin stitch and backstitch | 2 strands

Text
Maroon | Backstitch | 2 strands

TIP: Use a magnetic needle minder or needle box to always keep track of your needle when stitching, especially if you have pets or children around. Keep your curious dog or cat safe from ingesting embroidery floss by placing it in a sealable bag or out of reach while you're not using it.

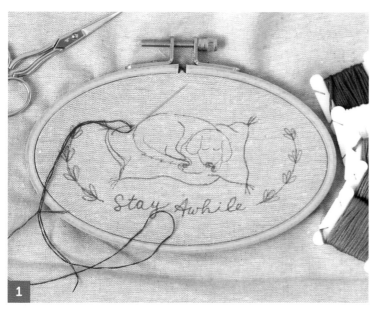

STEP 1: Prepare your materials. Following the tutorials in the Getting Started section, transfer your pattern, set your hoop, and separate your floss. Thread your needle with two strands of maroon floss.

STEP 2: Stitch the text "Stay Awhile." Using two strands of maroon floss, outline the text with backstitch. Keep your stitches very small in order to follow the curved letters.

STEP 3: Stitch the greenery branches. Using three strands of khaki-green floss, outline the branches with backstitch. Then, using the same floss, add three lazy daisy stitches to create each cluster of leaves on the branches.

Stay Awhile

STEP 4: Stitch the pillow. Using three strands of white floss, outline the pillow with backstitch. Use straight stitches to create the tassels at the corners of the pillow.

STEP 5: Stitch the dog. Using three strands of light-brown floss, outline the dog with backstitch. Try to keep your stitches short and equal in length in order to neatly follow the contours of the dog's shape.

4

5

STEP 6: Fill in the dog's paws and face. Using two strands of dark-gray floss, fill in the dog's nose and paw pads with two or three closely placed satin stitches. Use one stitch for each toe. Use three small backstitches to create the curved sleeping eyes of the dog.

STEP 7: Finish. Follow the steps on page 27 to finish the hoop. Remove any transfer pen marks as needed.

TIP: You can personalize this project by adding your dog's name in place of or below the text. Change out the color, adapt the ear shape of your dog, and add any other distinguishing features to make it your own. I stitched this one for my daughter's room; to make it extra cute, I added a floral crown on Daisy.

STITCH DIARY

"Because of the dog's joyfulness, our own is increased. It is no small gift. It is not the least reason why we should honor as well as love the dog of our own life, and the dog down the street, and all the dogs not yet born. What would the world be like without music or rivers or the green and tender grass? What would this world be like without dogs?"

—MARY OLIVER

Dogs, like good friends, provide us with loyal companionship, love, and support. When I think about some of the friendships of my life, I smile and am filled with gratitude. Being supported, encouraged, or comforted by a trustworthy friend during a difficult time, a joyful time, or as a part of our day-to-day lives is a true and beautiful gift.

Whether loyal dog or trusted human, in what ways has your closest companion supported and uplifted you during significant milestones or challenging times?

_____

_____

_____

_____

_____

_____

Sweater Weather

STITCHES

- Backstitch
- Lazy daisy
- Reverse chain stitch
- French knot

SUPPLIES

- 6" embroidery hoop
- 9" x 9" piece of your chosen fabric
- 1 skein of each floss color: dark gray, metallic gold, rose gold, light brown, ivory, mustard
- Embroidery scissors
- Embroidery needle
- Transfer materials (page 20)
- Finishing materials (page 26)
- Pattern (page 156)

I love waking up on a crisp, cool morning, after seemingly endless months of heat and humidity, and realizing it's finally time for one thing: sweater weather! In my humble opinion, autumn is hands down the best season of them all. I love the sun filtering through colorful leafy trees and all the familiar fall favorites like picking pumpkins, bonfires, and cozy nights in. This project pays homage to this time of year when we also get back to our comfortable, warm, and soft sweaters.

You can use any of the embroidery stitches you already know for filling in these dainty little sweaters, or you can follow my lead and try out two new stitches: reverse chain stitch and French knots. If you're new to either of these stitches, I recommend taking some time to practice them on a separate hooped piece of fabric. Take your time and enjoy learning these incredibly versatile stitches. As far as the colors and designs of the sweaters go, branch out and use your own color schemes, or follow my lead with the warm color palette I chose. Now it's time to indulge your inner fashion designer and stitch some sweaters! ■

QUICK REFERENCE

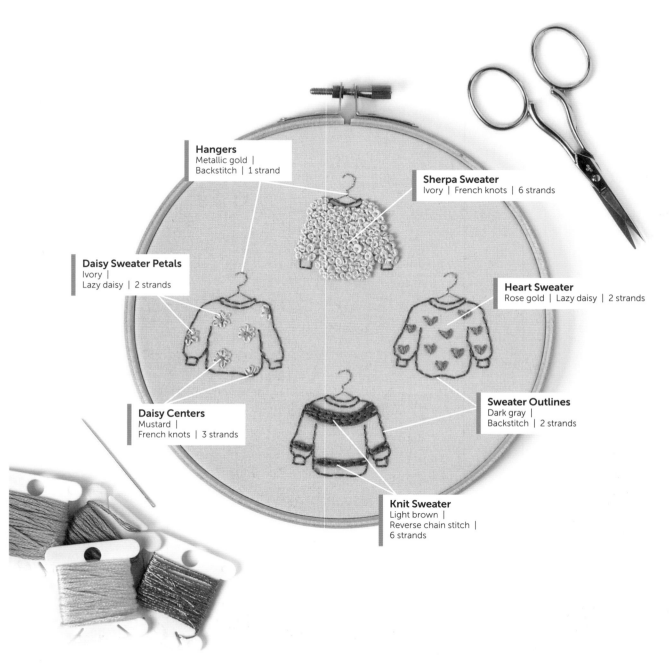

Hangers
Metallic gold |
Backstitch | 1 strand

Sherpa Sweater
Ivory | French knots | 6 strands

Daisy Sweater Petals
Ivory |
Lazy daisy | 2 strands

Heart Sweater
Rose gold | Lazy daisy | 2 strands

Daisy Centers
Mustard |
French knots | 3 strands

Sweater Outlines
Dark gray |
Backstitch | 2 strands

Knit Sweater
Light brown |
Reverse chain stitch |
6 strands

TIP: For the sweater at the bottom of this hoop, I chose to use reverse chain stitch to make it look knitted. If you're familiar with chain stitch, you'll see that it appears just the same. The difference is how the stitches are worked, and it's a matter of personal choice which stitch is easier for you. Feel free to use whichever you prefer.

STEP 1: Prepare your materials. Following the tutorials in the Getting Started section, transfer your pattern, set your hoop, and separate your floss. Thread your needle with two strands of dark-gray floss.

STEP 2: Stitch the sweaters. Using two strands of dark-gray floss, outline the sweaters with backstitch. For the Sherpa sweater on top, outline only the collar and wrists of the sweater.

STEP 3: Stitch the hangers. Using one strand of metallic-gold floss, outline the hangers with backstitch.

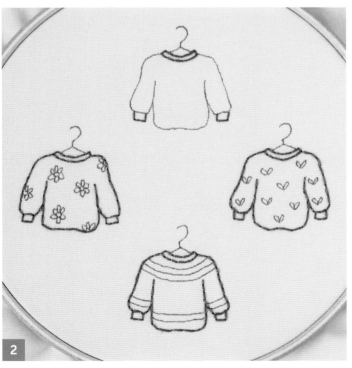

Sweater Weather

STEP 4: Stitch the heart sweater. Using two strands of rose-gold floss, stitch each heart with two lazy daisy stitches that meet at the bottom of the heart.

STEP 5: Stitch the knit sweater. Using six strands of light-brown floss, stitch two rows of reverse chain stitch. Start by making a small straight stitch, which serves as the anchor for the chain stitch. Then come up away from the stitch about ⅕" and guide your needle under the anchor stitch, but not through the fabric. Bring the needle back down though the fabric at the last entry point, creating a chain link secured by the initial anchor stitch. Now add another chain link by bringing your needle up through the fabric one stitch length away and guiding your needle under the first chain link. Bring the needle back down through the fabric at the entry point, creating a second chain link. Repeat, creating a row of chain stitch. Return to the same side of the sweater and add another row below the first one. Stitch a row of chain stitch on the sleeves of the sweater and across the bottom hem of the sweater.

STEP 6: Start the daisy sweater. Using two strands of ivory floss, make tiny lazy daisy stitches for each flower petal.

STEP 7: Finish the daisy sweater. Using three strands of mustard floss, make a French knot in the center of each daisy. Bring your needle up through the fabric in the center of the flower. With one hand, hold the floss perpendicular to the fabric, gripping it tightly a few inches above the fabric. With your other hand, place your needle against the back of the floss and hold it in place while you wrap the floss around it one time. With the looped floss on it, return your needle through the fabric just next to the starting point. Use one hand to hold the floss out to the side, keeping it taut. As you pull the needle through the fabric, gradually and steadily release the floss. You'll be left with a small yellow knot in the center of the flower.

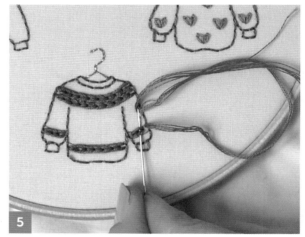

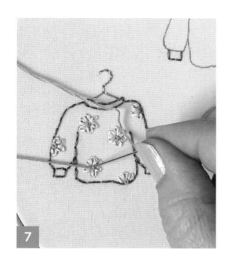

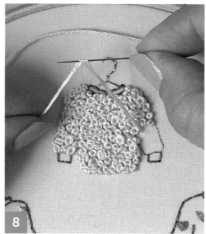

STEP 8: Fill in the Sherpa sweater. Using six strands of ivory floss, fill in the Sherpa sweater with closely spaced French knots. Wrap the floss around your needle one to three times to vary the size of the French knots.

STEP 9: Finish. Follow the steps on page 27 to finish the hoop. Remove any transfer pen marks as needed.

TIP: Think of how cute these sweaters would look styled for different seasons or holidays. Red and white for Christmas, pastels for spring, or orange, black, and creepy for Halloween!

STITCH DIARY

"Don't you love New York in the fall? It makes me wanna buy school supplies. I would send you a bouquet of newly sharpened pencils if I knew your name and address."
—JOE FOX, *You've Got Mail*

This quote from one of my favorite "comfort watch" movies, and these comfy little sweaters, makes me wish for fall! I'm so grateful for the change of seasons that we get to enjoy year-round. There is good to be found in every season, and each one makes us appreciate the next.

Take a moment to reflect on autumn, a season brimming with nature's transformative beauty. What sights, scents, or experiences do you look forward to when this season comes around?

_____

_____

_____

_____

_____

_____

_____

Let's Stay Home

STITCHES

- Reverse chain stitch
- Satin stitch
- French knot
- Backstitch
- Seed stitch
- Split backstitch

SUPPLIES

- 5" embroidery hoop
- 8" x 8" piece of your chosen fabric
- 1 skein of each floss color: blush, light mocha, light apricot, sage green, ivory
- Embroidery scissors
- Embroidery needle
- Transfer materials (page 20)
- Finishing materials (page 26)
- Pattern (page 157)

This one is for all my fellow happy homebodies! At the end of a long week, my favorite thing to do is perform a quick tidying up, order pizza, put on comfy pajamas, and settle in for a movie or board game night. I can rest knowing that my work is done for the week and truly relax and enjoy my family and my home.

I love the different textures used for each letter in this project, which gives you an opportunity to try out some new stitches or to employ your old favorites. Stick with the ones I've picked out for you, or take a look at the Stitch Library on page 144 to customize the way you outline or fill in your letters. Light a candle, put on my chill at-home playlist (found on page 10 and available on Apple Music), and spend some time with this short and simple project for your home. ■

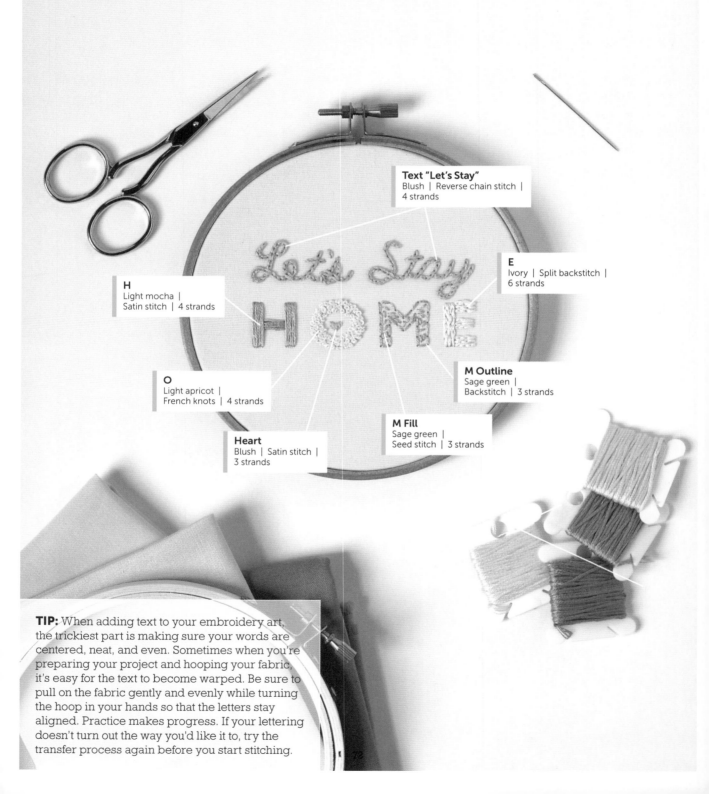

Text "Let's Stay"
Blush | Reverse chain stitch |
4 strands

E
Ivory | Split backstitch |
6 strands

H
Light mocha |
Satin stitch | 4 strands

M Outline
Sage green |
Backstitch | 3 strands

O
Light apricot |
French knots | 4 strands

M Fill
Sage green |
Seed stitch | 3 strands

Heart
Blush | Satin stitch |
3 strands

TIP: When adding text to your embroidery art, the trickiest part is making sure your words are centered, neat, and even. Sometimes when you're preparing your project and hooping your fabric, it's easy for the text to become warped. Be sure to pull on the fabric gently and evenly while turning the hoop in your hands so that the letters stay aligned. Practice makes progress. If your lettering doesn't turn out the way you'd like it to, try the transfer process again before you start stitching.

STEP 1: Prepare your materials. Following the tutorials in the Getting Started section, transfer your pattern, set your hoop, and separate your floss. Thread your needle with four strands of blush floss.

STEP 2: Stitch the text "Let's Stay." Using four strands of blush floss, outline the text with reverse chain stitch. Keep your stitches small in order to follow the curved letters. Note that you will start a new line of reverse chain stitch whenever you start a new lettering stroke or change direction—for example, when you cross the letter "t" and when you change direction at the top of the first "s."

STEP 3: Fill in the letter H. Using four strands of light-mocha floss, fill in the H with satin stitch. Individually fill in the three rectangles marked by the guidelines with vertical or horizontal stitches.

STEP 4: Fill in the letter O. Using four strands of light-apricot floss, fill in the O with French knots. Make your knots small and tight by wrapping the floss around your needle only one time and placing the knots closely together. Start by creating two rings of French knots just inside the outlines of the O, then fill in the middle.

STEP 5: Fill in the heart. Using three strands of blush floss, fill in the heart with satin stitch.

STEP 6: Stitch the letter M. Using three strands of sage-green floss, outline the letter M with backstitch. Make sure your stitches are short and uniform in length. Then, using the same floss, fill in the letter M with seed stitch. Seed stitch is done by simply sprinkling unconnected straight stitches to fill in a space.

STEP 7: Fill in the letter E. Using six strands of ivory floss, fill in the letter E with split backstitch. Use the guidelines on the pattern to separate the E into four individual rectangles. Fill in the first tall rectangle of the E with closely spaced vertical rows of split backstitch. Fill in the three remaining rectangles with closely spaced horizontal rows of split backstitch.

STEP 8: Finish. Follow the steps on page 27 to finish the hoop. Remove any transfer pen marks as needed.

TIP: For this project, I'm using a very lightweight cotton in a beautiful shade of pale blush. I'm using two layers of the fabric, like I often do, in order to help keep the tension in my fabric and avoid puckering. Using two layers of fabric also ensures the color is truer and more opaque. It can be a little more difficult to pull the floss through, but it is manageable, and the difficulty is outweighed by the end result!

76

STITCH DIARY

"Ah! There is nothing like staying at home, for real comfort."
—JANE AUSTEN

"Yes to love, yes to life, yes to staying in more!"
—LIZ LEMON, *30 Rock*

These two quotes from two of my biggest inspirations make me so glad to know we homebodies are in great company! There's nothing I love more than a night in with my family, and it's not just because at the end of the week I'm tired and would rather stay in. I love it because I want my two children to know our home is a place of warmth, comfort, security, and togetherness. Though my kids are young now, I hope at any age they will always want to hop on the couch for our Friday night pizza and movie tradition and know it is a place they can come as they are.

Describe your favorite type of night in. Are you someone who finds solace in being alone, or do you cherish spending the moment with someone special?

_____

_____

_____

_____

_____

_____

_____

Simple Countryside Bouquet

A handful of blush-pink daisies, fluffy cotton stems, and yellow wildflower buds make up this darling simple bouquet held together with a piece of baker's twine. This bouquet also features a handful of simple embroidery stitches that you've already learned with the previous projects in this book. Wondering how I created that dainty two-toned bow? It's an effect that looks complex but really is oh so simple. The useful and fun whipped backstitch is employed with two colors of floss to create the baker's twine, and I'll show you how with this project!

I used a piece of blush gingham cotton for the background of this cheerful piece to make it feel fit for a cottage home. You can swap out the gingham fabric for any color or print that coordinates with your home's décor style. You can also adapt the floss color palette to suit your style, making this a versatile floral bouquet embroidery project for anyone. ■

QUICK REFERENCE

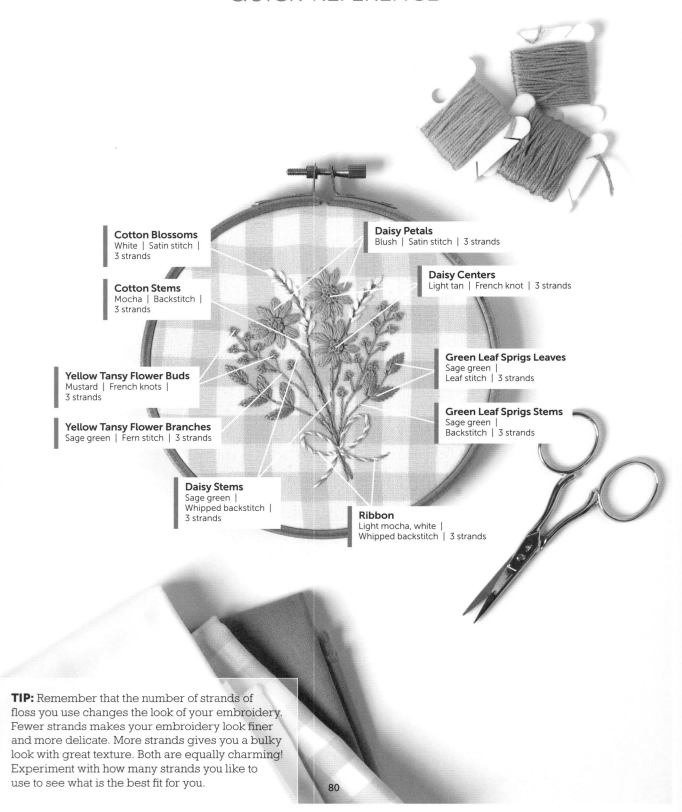

Cotton Blossoms
White | Satin stitch |
3 strands

Cotton Stems
Mocha | Backstitch |
3 strands

Yellow Tansy Flower Buds
Mustard | French knots |
3 strands

Yellow Tansy Flower Branches
Sage green | Fern stitch | 3 strands

Daisy Stems
Sage green |
Whipped backstitch |
3 strands

Daisy Petals
Blush | Satin stitch | 3 strands

Daisy Centers
Light tan | French knot | 3 strands

Green Leaf Sprigs Leaves
Sage green |
Leaf stitch | 3 strands

Green Leaf Sprigs Stems
Sage green |
Backstitch | 3 strands

Ribbon
Light mocha, white |
Whipped backstitch | 3 strands

TIP: Remember that the number of strands of floss you use changes the look of your embroidery. Fewer strands makes your embroidery look finer and more delicate. More strands gives you a bulky look with great texture. Both are equally charming! Experiment with how many strands you like to use to see what is the best fit for you.

STEP 1: Prepare your materials. Following the tutorials in the Getting Started section, transfer your pattern, set your hoop, and separate your floss. Thread your needle with three strands of sage-green floss.

STEP 2: Stitch the daisy flower stems. Using three strands of sage-green floss, outline the daisy flower stems in whipped backstitch.

STEP 3: Stitch the daisy petals. Using three strands of blush floss, fill in each flower petal with satin stitch. Start at the tip of each petal and end at the flower's center, keeping the stitches compact. Angle the outer stitches toward the center and overlap them slightly to fill in the shape of the petal. Repeat for each daisy petal.

Simple Countryside Bouquet

STEP 4: Stitch the flower centers. Using three strands of light-tan floss, fill in the flower centers with compact French knots (about 12 per flower center). Wrap the floss around your needle one to two times for each knot.

STEP 5: Stitch the cotton stems. Using three strands of mocha floss, outline the cotton stems with backstitch.

STEP 6: Stitch the cotton blossoms. Using three strands of white floss, add a cotton blossom to the stems with two or three closely placed satin stitches. Repeat for each blossom.

STEP 7: Stitch the branches. Using three strands of sage-green floss, outline the tansy flower branches with fern stitch. Then, using the same floss, outline the outer leaf sprig stems with backstitch.

STEP 8: Stitch the yellow tansy flowers. Using three strands of mustard floss, make a cluster of three French knots at the end of each tansy branch. Wrap the floss around your needle one to two times to make small, tidy flower buds. Repeat for each cluster of flower buds.

STEP 9: Stitch the leaves. Using three strands of sage-green floss, fill in the leaves with leaf stitch. Start with one straight stitch down the center of the leaf, from the leaf's tip to about three-quarters of the way to the base. Start the second stitch by bringing the needle out on the top left side of the first stitch at the edge of the leaf. Cross over the first stitch, ending just to its right in the middle of the leaf. Repeat on the opposite side of the leaf. Continue stitching to the base of the leaf, keeping your stitches parallel to one another on each side. Fill in each leaf with this method.

STEP 10: Begin stitching the ribbon. Using three strands of light-mocha floss, outline the ribbon with backstitch. (This is the first half of the whipped backstitch that will create the final effect.)

STEP 11: Finish stitching the ribbon. Using three strands of white floss, complete outlining the light-mocha ribbon with whipped backstitch.

STEP 12: Finish. Follow the steps on page 27 to finish the hoop. Remove any transfer pen marks as needed.

TIP: The centers of the daisies can be stitched with different types of stitches. The fluffy look, pictured in the hoop on the right, is achieved with turkey work stitch, described in the Blush Meadow Abstract project on page 130 and in the Stitch Library on page 148.

84

STITCH DIARY

"To be thrilled by the stars at night; to be elated over a bird's nest or a wildflower in spring—these are some of the rewards of the simple life."
—JOHN BURROUGHS

The gentle beauty of the countryside, a warm cup of peppermint tea on a cold night, the delicious smell of homemade chocolate chip cookies baking in the oven, adding the finishing stitch to a piece of embroidery: these are some of my favorite little things. These simple, quiet pleasures, whether we view them as mundane or beautiful, become the fabric of our lives.

**List some of your favorite
simple rewards or pleasures in life.**

_____

_____

_____

_____

_____

_____

_____

Starry Night

STITCHES

- Whipped backstitch
- Satin stitch
- Straight stitch
- Fern stitch
- Long and short stitch

SUPPLIES

- 5" embroidery hoop
- 8" x 8" piece of your chosen fabric
- 1 skein of each floss color: light brown, ivory, metallic gold, mauve, light pine green, beige, soft blue, light gray
- Embroidery scissors
- Embroidery needle
- Transfer materials (page 20)
- Finishing materials (page 26)
- Pattern (page 159)

A cozy vantage point for stargazing on a clear night with a curious and charming furry friend—it's a cat lover's dream! We'll be using an excellent fill stitch called long and short stitch and a technique called thread painting to fill in this cat's fur coat. Thread-painted embroidery uses one or two strands of straight stitches or long and short stitches, building layer upon layer to create a desired color and natural-looking effects. This is what makes beautiful embroidered animal portraits or landscape scenes look very realistic. Spending some time stitching this cat can serve as a test to see if thread painting is something you're interested in.

As you fill in the body of the cat, think like a painter and imagine each stitch is a single brushstroke. Carefully place each stitch in the direction that cat fur would naturally lie. Typically, you'll want to choose three or four hues of the same color to blend and mimic animal fur, but, for this project, we'll start with simply using one color. Select any white, tan, black, or gray floss color for your feline friend, or customize your cat to be a tabby, calico, or Siamese with a few different shades of floss in varying patterns. ■

QUICK REFERENCE

Window Frame
Light brown | Satin stitch | 4 strands

Window Lines
Light brown | Whipped backstitch | 4 strands

Moon
Ivory | Satin stitch | 3 strands

Stars
Metallic gold | Straight stitch | 1 strand

Plant
Light pine green | Fern stitch | 3 strands

Cat
Light gray | Long and short stitch | 2 strands

Plant Container
Ivory | Satin stitch | 3 strands

Books
Mauve, light pine green, beige, soft blue | Satin stitch | 3 strands

TIP: Getting a smooth satin stitch is key in this design. Separating your floss into individual strands and then bringing them back together before threading your needle is what will help you achieve this look.

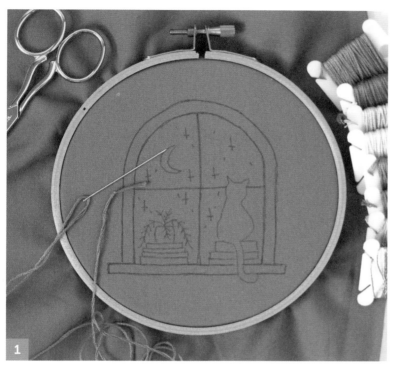

STEP 1: Prepare your materials.
Following the tutorials in the Getting Started section, transfer your pattern, set your hoop, and separate your floss. Thread your needle with four strands of light-brown floss.

STEP 2: Stitch the window lines.
Using four strands of light-brown floss, outline the lines between the windowpanes with whipped backstitch.

STEP 3: Fill in the window frame and sill.
Using four strands of light-brown floss, fill in the windowsill with satin stitch. Then fill in the arched window frame with satin stitch. Create guidelines with floss about ½" apart and work on filling in one section at a time. This will help you keep your satin stitches parallel and uniform.

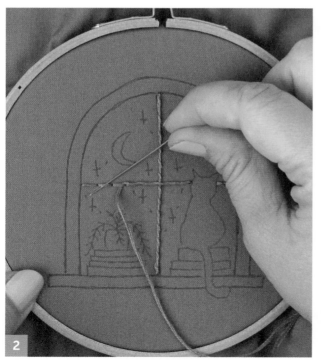

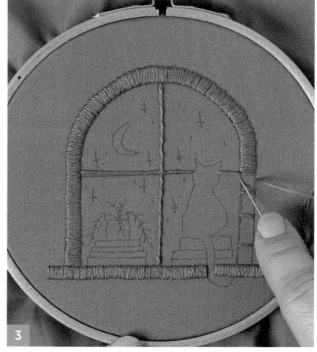

Starry Night

STEP 4: Fill in the moon. Using three strands of ivory floss, fill in the moon with satin stitch.

STEP 5: Add the stars. Using one strand of metallic-gold floss, stitch the stars with straight stitch. Start with one vertical stitch and cross it with one horizontal stitch. For the small stars, stitch one tiny straight stitch.

STEP 6: Stitch the book stacks. Using three strands of mauve floss, fill in the first book with satin stitch. Then, using three strands of light-pine green, beige, and soft-blue floss, fill in the remaining books with satin stitch.

STEP 7: Stitch the plant pot. Using three strands of ivory floss, fill in the plant pot with satin stitch.

STEP 8: Stitch the plant. Using three strands of light-pine-green floss, outline the plant with fern stitch.

STEP 9: Fill in the cat. Using two strands of light-gray floss, fill the cat with long and short stitch. Start at the ears and work down toward the tail, following the contours of the cat. To fill in the ears, make a few closely spaced straight stitches, angled in and overlapping to meet at the tops of the ears. Then begin filling in the head and body of the cat

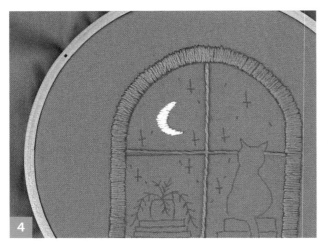

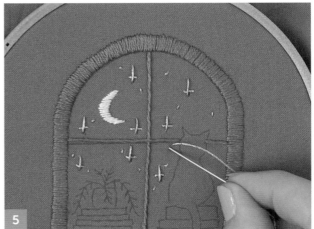

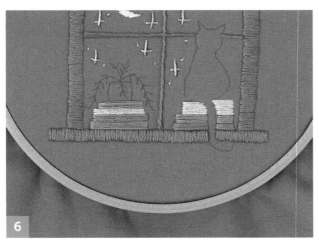

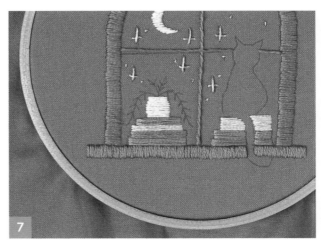

with long and short stitch. Stitch a row of compact straight stitches with alternating lengths of ¼" and ⅛". The next row will be stitched directly below it with stitches of the same length (¼"). Repeat adding rows of these same-length stitches until the cat is filled in entirely. Don't be afraid to wedge in an extra stitch here or there to fill in the gaps and to create a natural-looking fur coat.

STEP 10: Finish. Follow the steps on page 27 to finish the hoop. Remove any transfer pen marks as needed.

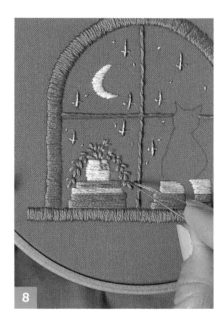

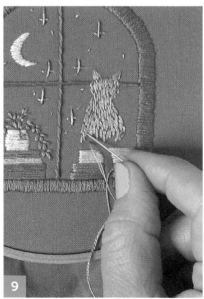

TIP: Adding small crystals or beads is a way to add dimension, sparkle, and shine to your embroidery, as you can see in the bottom piece shown here. Take a look at the beading aisle in your local craft store and see what catches your attention. You can easily add beads to the surface of your embroidery with a beading or thin needle and a small straight stitch.

STITCH DIARY

*"I love cats because I enjoy my home; and little by little,
they become its visible soul."*
—JEAN COCTEAU

Cats can give a home character or a soul, bringing it joy or tranquility,
playfulness or calm, and make us feel more at home. But the soul of a home
comes from other things too, like design, color, and style. You can intentionally
curate your home to evoke certain feelings and support what's important to you.
For example, do you want your home to be calm and restful or bright
and cheerful? Your home doesn't have to be perfect to start. Begin small,
like dressing up a window nook with a cozy chair, your favorite books,
art, plants, and a basket of soft blankets.

**Whether or not you share your home with a cat,
what is the soul of your home like? List what makes
your home unique and comforting to you.**

_____

_____

_____

_____

_____

_____

Cozy Cottage

STITCHES

- Whipped backstitch
- Long and short stitch
- Backstitch
- Straight stitch
- Woven wheel
- French knot
- Lazy daisy
- Satin stitch
- Leaf stitch
- Fern stitch

SUPPLIES

- 6" embroidery hoop
- 9" x 9" piece of your chosen fabric
- 1 skein of each floss color: ivory, mocha, pale pink, rose gold, khaki green, beige, blush, maroon
- Embroidery scissors
- Embroidery needle
- Transfer materials (page 20)
- Finishing materials (page 26)
- Pattern (page 160)

Create an adorable cozy cottage covered in flowers while exploring a wide variety of stitches with this project. Wouldn't you love to spend time in such a whimsical little cottage?

Something that might stand out to you, literally, is the addition of the three-dimensional woven-wheel roses at the base of this cottage. These roses might look complicated, but don't be intimidated. You'll be surprised at how easily they are formed. If you're interested in more stitches to add dimension to your embroidery, take a look into the art of stumpwork, or raised three-dimensional embroidery, to explore dozens of unique stitches and techniques to bring your embroidery to life. But first, grab your embroidery supplies and let's stitch this cozy cottage together! ■

QUICK REFERENCE

Leaf Trio Leaves
Khaki green | Leaf stitch | 6 strands
Leaf Trio Branches
Mocha | Backstitch | 6 strands

Simple Branches
Maroon, blush |
Fern stitch | 3 strands

Wildflowers
Ivory | Satin stitch | 4 strands
Wildflower Stems
Khaki green | Backstitch | 4 strands

Door and Balcony
Mocha | Backstitch | 6 strands

Large Half-Daisy Petals
Ivory | Satin stitch | 6 strands
Large Half-Daisy Center
Rose gold | French knots | 4 strands

Berry Branches
Mocha | Fern stitch | 4 strands
Berries
Maroon | French knots | 6 strands

Cottage Outline
Ivory | Whipped backstitch |
6 strands
Roof
Mocha | Long and short stitch |
6 strands

Small Half-Daisy Petals
Blush | Satin stitch | 6 strands
Small Half-Daisy Center
Pale pink | French knots | 4 strands

Cottage Details
Ivory | Straight stitch | 6 strands

Roses
Pale pink, rose gold |
Woven wheel | 6 strands
Rose Centers
Pale pink, rose gold |
French knots | 4 strands
Rose Accent Flowers
Blush | Lazy daisy | 6 strands

Large Leaf Sprigs
Khaki green | Lazy daisy, backstitch | 6 strands

Large Window
Ivory | Whipped backstitch | 4 strands
Small Windows
Ivory | Whipped backstitch | 3 strands
Windowpanes and Doorknob
Ivory | Backstitch | 3 strands

Ground Daisies Petals
Beige | Satin stitch | 4 strands
Ground Daisies Centers
Blush | Satin stitch | 3 strands
Ground Filler Leaves
Khaki green | Leaf stitch | 4 strands

Path
Mocha | Straight stitch | 6 strands

TIP: When weaving your woven-wheel roses, try not to catch the floss with the sharp end of your needle. If it helps, you can actually weave with the eye end of the needle and achieve the same effect without any loose strands of floss being caught.

STEP 1: Prepare your materials. Following the tutorials in the Getting Started section, transfer your pattern, set your hoop, and separate your floss. Thread your needle with six strands of ivory floss.

STEP 2: Stitch the cottage outline. Using six strands of ivory floss, outline the three edges of the cottage with whipped backstitch.

STEP 3: Stitch the roof. Using six strands of mocha floss, outline the roof with two parallel rows of long and short stitch, meeting at the point.

STEP 4: Stitch the windows. Using four strands of ivory floss, outline the large window with whipped backstitch. Then outline the three smaller windows with three strands of whipped backstitch. Finally, using three strands of ivory floss, outline all the windowpanes with backstitch.

Cozy Cottage

STEP 5: Stitch the door and the balcony. Using six strands of mocha floss, outline the door and the balcony with backstitch. Then, using three strands of ivory floss, add the doorknob with one tiny backstitch.

STEP 6: Stitch the cottage details. Using six strands of ivory floss, stitch the cottage detail lines with straight stitch.

STEP 7: Stitch the sidewalk path. Using six strands of mocha floss, stitch the path with straight stitches. Stitch each path element once, then add another

stitch of the same size over the top of each element to make each stitch more full.

STEP 8: Stitch the roses. Using six strands of pale-pink floss, add the woven-wheel rose in the left corner of the cottage. Start by stitching the five spokes using straight stitch. Then bring the needle up near the center of the spokes and alternate weaving over and under the spokes repeatedly around the circle, building layers. Return the needle back through the fabric once the rose is full. Then, using four strands of rose-gold floss, add French knots to the center of the rose. Wrap the floss

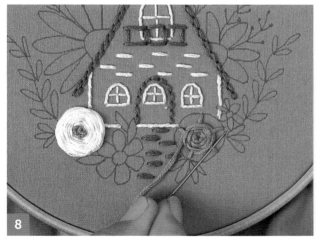

around your needle two times for each French knot. Repeat this method to make the second rose on the right of the cottage, using rose-gold floss for the rose and pale-pink floss for the French knots in the center.

STEP 9: Stitch the large leaf sprigs. Using six strands of khaki-green floss, backstitch the centerline of the branch. Then, using the same floss, add lazy daisy stitches along the centerline to create the leaves. Repeat this for the second large leaf sprig.

STEP 10: Stitch the daisies. Using four strands of beige floss, fill in the petals of the two daisies with satin stitch. Then, using three strands of blush floss, fill in the centers of the daisies with satin stitch.

STEP 11: Stitch the rose accent flowers. Using six strands of blush floss, stitch the rose accent flowers with lazy daisy stitches.

STEP 12: Fill in the leaves. Using four strands of khaki-green floss, fill in the leaves around the flowers at the base of the cottage with leaf stitch.

Cozy Cottage

STEP 13: Stitch the large half daisy on the left side of the roof. Using six strands of ivory floss, fill in the daisy petals with satin stitch. Start at the tip of the petal, stitching in toward the center, and allow your stitches to slightly overlap at the base of the petal. The stitches at the outer edges of the petals will slightly angle inward to form the shape of the petals. Then, using four strands of rose-gold floss, fill in the center of the daisy with French knots. Wrap the floss around your needle two times for each French knot.

STEP 14: Stitch the small half daisy on the right side of the roof. Using six strands of blush floss, fill in the daisy petals with satin stitch. Use the same method for filling in the petals as in step 13. Then, using four strands of pale-pink floss, fill in the center of the daisy with French knots. Wrap the floss around your needle two times for each French knot.

STEP 15: Stitch the simple branches. Using three strands of maroon floss, stitch the simple branches by the ivory daisy with fern stitch. Then, using three strands of blush floss, stitch the simple branches near the top of the roof with fern stitch.

STEP 16: Stitch the leaf trio. Using six strands of khaki-green floss, fill in the leaf trio with leaf stitch. Then, using six strands of mocha floss, backstitch the leaf trio branches.

STEP 17: Stitch the wildflowers. Using four strands of khaki-green floss, backstitch the flower stems. Then, using four strands of ivory floss, fill in the flowers with satin stitch.

STEP 18: Stitch the berry branches. Using four strands of mocha floss, stitch the berry branches with fern stitch. Then, using six strands of maroon floss, add a French knot to the end of each branch as a berry.

STEP 19: Finish. Follow the steps on page 27 to finish the hoop. Remove any transfer pen marks as needed.

19

TIP: Stitch this piece as a housewarming gift for a loved one and add their family name and a special date at the bottom of the hoop.

STITCH DIARY

"You can have more than one home. You can carry your roots with you, and decide where they grow."
—HENNING MANKELL

Until my 30th birthday, I had lived in the same area all my life, but that year we decided to leave behind the familiarity of our home in Illinois and embark on a new chapter of life in Austin, Texas. It was such a monumental challenge for me to leave everything I had ever known for a place where I knew no one! With an open mind and heart, I set out to make new friends, and, sure enough, over time we found community and our new surroundings evolved to feel like home. Yet anytime I visit my parents and step foot in the place I grew up, I also have that unmistakable feeling of home, which makes me realize that home can exist in more than one place.

Look back on the locations that life has taken you and write about the places that have been home for you. Reflect on what made each one special.

_____

_____

_____

_____

_____

_____

Winter Botanicals

STITCHES

- Satin stitch
- French knot
- Leaf stitch
- Backstitch
- Fern stitch
- Whipped backstitch
- Straight stitch

SUPPLIES

- 7" embroidery hoop
- 10" x 10" piece of your chosen fabric
- 1 skein of each floss color: light apricot, beige, white, dark gray, sage green, light jade, mauve, medium blue, ivory, mocha, khaki green
- Embroidery scissors
- Embroidery needle
- Transfer materials (page 20)
- Finishing materials (page 26)
- Pattern (page 161)

So often when we think of flowers, what comes to mind are tulips, poppies, cosmos, or other cheerful and bright flowers that bloom during the spring and summer months. But the botanicals in this project are inspired by cold-weather favorites, such as evergreens, anemones, pine cones, juniper berries, and more. I hope this piece reminds you to look for and embrace the beauty in all seasons!

A floral piece like this one can be a great way to experiment with a color palette. I chose a wintry earth-toned palette of soft whites with small pops of color against a contrasting deep-green background. If you don't have a deep-green fabric on hand, I suggest trying another muted earth tone, like oatmeal, taupe, or even a soft blue to capture the delicate beauty of these winter botanicals. Feel free to showcase another color palette if you'd like, with red or pink anemones and winter berries. Or take a look at some basic color theory described on page 151 to learn more about the art and science of floss color selection. ■

QUICK REFERENCE

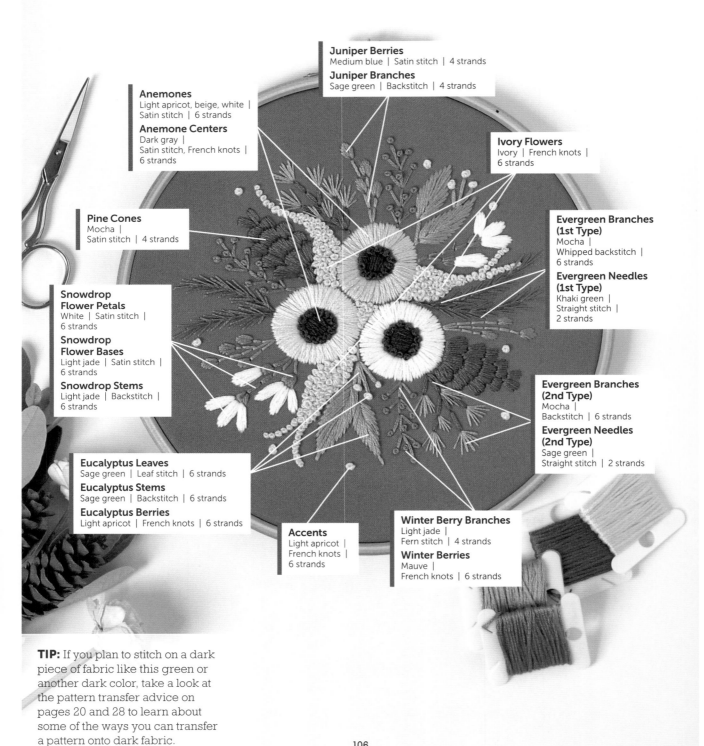

Juniper Berries
Medium blue | Satin stitch | 4 strands
Juniper Branches
Sage green | Backstitch | 4 strands

Anemones
Light apricot, beige, white |
Satin stitch | 6 strands
Anemone Centers
Dark gray |
Satin stitch, French knots |
6 strands

Ivory Flowers
Ivory | French knots |
6 strands

Pine Cones
Mocha |
Satin stitch | 4 strands

**Evergreen Branches
(1st Type)**
Mocha |
Whipped backstitch |
6 strands
**Evergreen Needles
(1st Type)**
Khaki green |
Straight stitch |
2 strands

**Snowdrop
Flower Petals**
White | Satin stitch |
6 strands
**Snowdrop
Flower Bases**
Light jade | Satin stitch |
6 strands
Snowdrop Stems
Light jade | Backstitch |
6 strands

**Evergreen Branches
(2nd Type)**
Mocha |
Backstitch | 6 strands
**Evergreen Needles
(2nd Type)**
Sage green |
Straight stitch | 2 strands

Eucalyptus Leaves
Sage green | Leaf stitch | 6 strands
Eucalyptus Stems
Sage green | Backstitch | 6 strands
Eucalyptus Berries
Light apricot | French knots | 6 strands

Accents
Light apricot |
French knots |
6 strands

Winter Berry Branches
Light jade |
Fern stitch | 4 strands
Winter Berries
Mauve |
French knots | 6 strands

TIP: If you plan to stitch on a dark piece of fabric like this green or another dark color, take a look at the pattern transfer advice on pages 20 and 28 to learn about some of the ways you can transfer a pattern onto dark fabric.

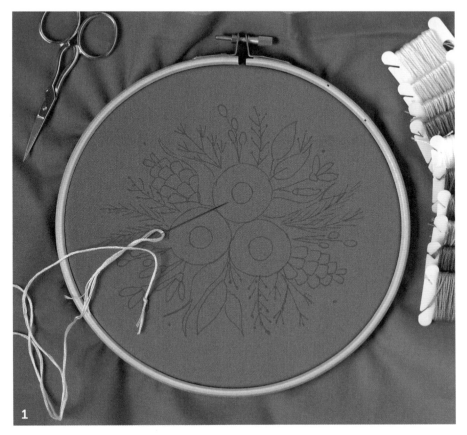

STEP 1: Prepare your materials. Following the tutorials in the Getting Started section, transfer your pattern, set your hoop, and separate your floss. Thread your needle with six strands of light-apricot floss.

STEP 2: Stitch the anemones. Using six strands of light-apricot floss, satin-stitch the anemone at the left center of the design. Before filling in the flower, stitch several spokes around the center to guide your stitches. As you fill in the flower, some of your stitches will overlap at the center. Repeat this method for the remaining two anemones, using six strands of beige floss for the top anemone and six strands of white floss for the bottom anemone.

STEP 3: Fill in the anemone centers. Use six strands of dark-gray floss to fill in the center circles of each anemone with satin stitch. Then add a ring of French knots around each center circle. For the French knots, use six strands of dark-gray floss and wrap the floss around your needle twice so that each French knot slightly overlaps the center and the petals.

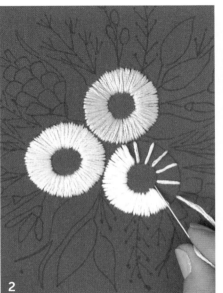

STEP 4: Stitch the eucalyptus leaves and stems. Use six strands of sage-green floss to fill in the eucalyptus leaves with leaf stitch. Then, using the same floss, outline the stems with backstitch.

STEP 5: Add the eucalyptus berries. Using six strands of light-apricot floss, make French knots for the berries. Wrap the floss around your needle two times for each berry.

STEP 6: Fill in the snowdrop petals. Using six strands of white floss, satin-stitch the snowdrop petals. Start with one stitch down the center of each petal from tip to base, then fill in each side with nearly parallel stitches. To avoid crowding at the base of each petal, end some of the stitches just before the base and lightly overlap others.

STEP 7: Stitch the snowdrop flower bases and stems. Using six strands of light-jade floss, satin-stitch the bases of each flower. Then, using the same floss, backstitch the stems.

STEP 8: Stitch the winter berries. Using four strands of light-jade floss, outline the berry branches with fern stitch. Then, using six strands of mauve floss, add a French knot to the end of each branch. Wrap the floss around your needle one time for each berry.

STEP 9: Stitch the juniper berries. Using four strands of medium-blue floss, fill in the juniper berries with satin stitch. Angle and overlap the outer stitches to fit the shape of the berries. Then, using four strands of sage-green floss, backstitch the juniper branches.

STEP 10: Stitch the ivory flowers. Using six strands of ivory floss, fill in the ivory flowers with compact French knots. Start by outlining each flower shape with a row of French knots, then fill in the centers of the shapes. Wrap the floss around your needle one or two times for each French knot.

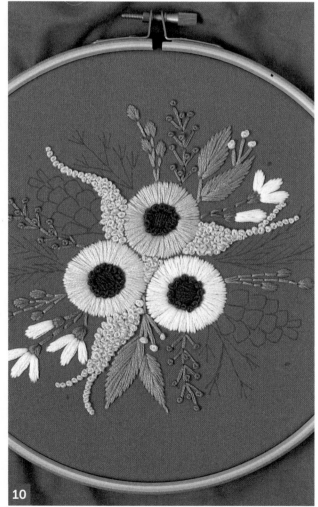

STEP 11: Stitch the first type of evergreen branches. Using six strands of mocha floss, outline the evergreen branches with whipped backstitch. Then, using two strands of khaki-green floss, outline the evergreen needles with straight stitch.

STEP 12: Stitch the second type of evergreen branches. Using six strands of mocha floss, outline the evergreen branches with backstitch. Then, using two strands of sage-green floss, outline the evergreen needles with straight stitch.

STEP 13: Fill in the pine cones. Using four strands of mocha floss, satin-stitch each section of the pine cones.

STEP 14: Add the accents. Using six strands of light-apricot floss, add French knot accents wherever a dot is shown on the pattern. Wrap the floss around your needle two times for each French knot.

STEP 15: Finish. Follow the steps on page 27 to finish the hoop. Remove any transfer pen marks as needed.

TIP: You can trace elements of this design onto cloth napkins, sweaters, or hand towels to create special pieces of embroidery for gifts or for your home. For items being taken out of the hoop, I recommend using very short stitches to reduce the likelihood of the floss being snagged during use.

STITCH DIARY

*"Winter is the time for comfort, for good food
and warmth, for the touch of a friendly hand, and for a talk
beside the fire: it is the time for home."*
—EDITH SITWELL

Have you noticed that nature reflects the changes in your life? You can
take cues from nature and its changes and draw meaning from the seasons.
For example, in a season of personal growth, a field of blooming spring wildflowers
comes to mind. In a season of happiness and excitement, you might envision
a warm summer day. In a season of change, you might imagine a tree
shedding its leaves in the fall. In a season of introspection and stillness,
imagine a forest in hibernation during the winter.

**Reflect on different seasons of your life,
each a unique chapter with its own beauty and significance.
Describe the season you currently find yourself in.**

_____

_____

_____

_____

_____

_____

Booked All Weekend

STITCHES

- Fern stitch
- Satin stitch
- Backstitch
- Straight stitch
- French knot
- Split backstitch
- Leaf stitch
- Reverse chain stitch
- Lazy daisy

SUPPLIES

- 7" embroidery hoop
- 10" x 10" piece of your chosen fabric
- 1 skein of each floss color: bright green, terra-cotta, forest green, pale blush, mustard, light jade, blush, light gray, sage green, ivory, light tan, light mocha, light brown, brown
- Embroidery scissors
- Embroidery needle
- Transfer materials (page 20)
- Finishing materials (page 26)
- Pattern (page 162)

If you love tiny details, this is the project for you! This embroidery piece, inspired by relaxing hobbies and taking "me time," is perfect for getting acquainted with your Embroidery Stitch Library, found on page 144. You'll see how mixing in a few different stitches adds texture and detail that make a big impact.

You can work on this piece from left to right, from top to bottom, or by jumping around and working on any element of your choice. But do pay attention to the way you stitch a motif with multiple colors—a potted plant, for example. I recommend that you stitch the plant first and then the pot. Then, once all the items on a shelf are stitched, stitch the shelf on which they sit. Basically, you'll want to start with the parts farthest in the background in the design and work your way to the foreground so that any overlapping looks natural and prevents you from disrupting layers that have been already stitched. ■

QUICK REFERENCE

Books
Terra-cotta, blush, forest green, light tan | Satin stitch | 4 strands

Teacup
Ivory | Backstitch, satin stitch | 4 strands

Teabag Label
Ivory | Satin stitch | 4 strands

Teabag String and Steam
Light gray | Backstitch | 3 strands

Books
Forest green, pale blush, mustard, light jade, blush | Satin stitch | 4 strands

Plant
Bright green | Fern stitch | 4 strands

Pot
Terra-cotta | Satin stitch | 4 strands

Flame
Mustard | Satin stitch | 4 strands

Candle
Pale blush, bright green | Satin stitch | 4 strands

Outline
Light gray | Backstitch | 4 strands

Stems
Sage green | Backstitch | 4 strands

Florets
Blush | Straight stitch | 6 strands

Vase
Light gray | Backstitch | 4 strands

Books
Ivory, light tan, forest green | Satin stitch | 4 strands

Embroidery Section 1
Pale blush | Satin stitch | 3 strands

Embroidery Section 2
Blush | Satin stitch | 3 strands

Embroidery Section 3
Light mocha | French knots | 3 strands

Embroidery Section 4
Light mocha | Satin stitch | 3 strands

Embroidery Section 5
Pale blush | Split backstitch | 3 strands

Wooden Circle
Light brown | Split backstitch | 6 strands

Fastener
Light tan | Straight stitch | 2 strands

Shelves
Light brown | Split backstitch | 6 strands

Books
Light tan, mustard, light jade, pale blush, forest green, brown | Satin stitch | 4 strands

Plant
Light jade | Leaf stitch | 4 strands

Pot
Blush | Split backstitch | 6 strands

Books
Blush, brown, mustard, ivory, light tan | Satin stitch | 4 strands

Plant
Sage green, bright green | Satin stitch | 4 strands

Pot
Ivory | Satin stitch | 4 strands

Yarn
Ivory, mustard, blush, light jade | Satin stitch | 4 strands

Basket Handles
Light mocha | Split backstitch | 6 strands

Basket
Light mocha | Reverse chain stitch | 6 strands

Books
Blush, pale blush, light tan | Satin stitch | 4 strands

Bud Vases
Brown | Satin stitch | 3 strands

Yellow Flower Stems
Bright green | Straight stitch | 3 strands

Yellow Flowers
Mustard | French knots | 4 strands

Leafy Stem Stem
Sage green | Backstitch | 3 strands

Leafy Stem Leaves
Sage green | Lazy daisy | 3 strands

TIP: Remember to take care of yourself while stitching. It can be so easy to get lost in a fun project like this one as the hours tick by. I recommend taking frequent breaks and checking on your posture. Be sure you have adequate lighting so you don't strain your eyes. If you find your wrists need a break from gripping your embroidery hoop, you might want to invest in an embroidery hoop stand, found at any craft store or online.

STEP 1: Prepare your materials. Following the tutorials in the Getting Started section, transfer your pattern, set your hoop, and separate your floss. Thread your needle with four strands of bright-green floss. We'll start with the top left corner of the shelves and work our way over and down through the rows. Feel free to skip around to any items on the shelves as you wish.

STEP 2: Stitch the top left potted plant. Using four strands of bright-green floss, outline the plant with fern stitch. Using four strands of terra-cotta floss, fill in the body of the pot with vertical satin stitches, slightly angling the stitches at the sides of the pot. Then use horizontal stitches for the top and bottom of the pot, overlapping the vertical stitches to cover their ends.

STEP 3: Stitch the first cluster of books. Using four strands of forest-green floss, fill in the first book with satin stitch. Then stitch the next books using four strands of pale-blush, mustard, light-jade, and blush floss. Add a small contrasting stripe consisting of two horizontal satin stitches across the spines of the pale-blush and the light-jade books with blush floss.

Booked All Weekend

STEP 4: Stitch the candle. Using four strands of mustard floss, fill in the candle flame with satin stitch. Using four strands of bright-green floss, fill in the candle label with satin stitch. Then, using four strands of pale-blush floss, fill in the candle jar with satin stitch. Finally, using four strands of light-gray floss, outline the candle with backstitch.

STEP 5: Stitch the flowers in the glass vase. Using four strands of sage-green floss, outline the flower stems with backstitch. Then, using six strands of blush floss, add the florets with two straight stitches each. First make one straight stitch and then another directly on top of it to give the florets more dimension. Then, using four strands of light-gray floss, outline the glass vase and waterline with backstitch.

STEP 6: Stitch the stack of books. Using four strands of ivory floss, fill in the bottom book with satin stitch. Then repeat for the remaining two books with light-tan and forest-green floss.

STEP 7: Stitch the stack of books and teacup. Move to the second shelf. Using four strands of terra-cotta floss, fill in the bottom book with satin stitch. Repeat for the second and third books using four strands of blush floss and forest-green floss. Add a contrasting stripe on the blush

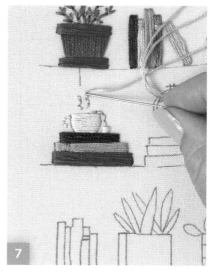

book with four strands of light-tan floss. Next, fill in the teacup using four strands of ivory floss with satin stitch. Backstitch the handle of the teacup using the same floss. Then, using the same floss again, fill in the square teabag label with a few satin stitches. Outline the teabag

string in backstitch using three strands of light-gray floss. Finally, using the same floss, outline the steam lines above the teacup in backstitch.

STEP 8: Stitch the embroidery art. Feel free to get creative and use your choice of colors and

Then, using six strands of light-brown floss, outline the wooden circle in split backstitch. Last, use two strands of light-tan floss to outline the fastener at the top of the hoop with straight stitch.

STEP 9: Stitch the next row of books. Using four strands of light-tan floss, satin-stitch the bottom book lying on the shelf. Use four strands of mustard floss to add a contrasting stripe to the spine of the book. Then, using four strands of floss, satin-stitch the remaining books in the following colors: light jade, pale blush, forest green (with a pale-blush stripe), brown, light jade (with a light-tan stripe), forest green, pale blush, mustard, brown (with a light-tan stripe), and pale blush.

STEP 10: Stitch the potted plant. Using four strands of light-jade floss, fill in the plant with leaf stitch. Then, using six strands of blush floss, fill in the basket with rows of split backstitch.

STEP 11: Stitch the next row of books. Move to the third shelf. Using four strands of blush floss, satin-stitch the first book and add a contrasting stripe with four strands of ivory floss. Continue filling in the books with four strands of brown, mustard, ivory (with light-tan stripes), and light-tan floss.

stitches for this part, or follow these steps to make yours look just like the sample. Using three strands of pale-blush floss, fill in the top left section with vertical satin stitches. Using three strands of blush floss, fill in the section below the first with horizontal satin stitches. Using three strands

of light-mocha floss, fill in the section to the right of that with small, closely spaced French knots. Using three strands of light-mocha floss, fill in the bottom left section with horizontal satin stitches. Using three strands of pale-blush floss, fill in the final section with split backstitch.

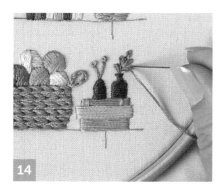

STEP 12: Stitch the potted plant. Using four strands of sage-green floss, satin-stitch two of the leaves. Start at the top point of each leaf and end the stitch at the top of the flowerpot. Angle the stitches on the edge to fit the shape of the leaf. Repeat this process by using four strands of bright-green floss for the remaining leaves. Then, using four strands of ivory floss, satin-stitch the flowerpot.

STEP 13: Stitch the basket of yarn. Using four strands of ivory floss, satin-stitch two of the balls of yarn. Start by stitching across the entire circle, then add another partial layer of satin stitches lying in a contrasting direction to create the look of a ball of yarn. Repeat this process with mustard, blush, and light jade. Then, using six strands of light-mocha floss, outline the basket handles with split backstitch. Finally, using the same floss, fill in the body of the basket with horizontal rows of reverse chain stitch.

STEP 14: Stitch the final book stack and bud vases. Using four strands of blush floss, satin-stitch the bottom book. Then satin-stitch the second book with four strands of pale-blush floss. Satin-stitch the top book with four strands of light-tan floss and add a contrasting stripe to it with blush floss. Next, satin-stitch the bud vases with three strands of brown floss. Using three strands of bright-green floss, straight-stitch the flower stems on the left. Add a French knot to the top of each stem using four strands of mustard floss. Finally, backstitch the second stem using three strands of sage-green floss and add a lazy daisy stitch using three strands for each of the five leaves.

STEP 15: Stitch the bookshelves. Before you begin stitching the shelves, check that your fabric is taut and that the shelf lines are straight. Adjust your fabric as needed and use the weave of your fabric to help guide you in stitching your shelves as straight as possible. Remember that you can erase your pattern transfer lines when you're finished. Using six strands of light-brown floss, make a row of split backstitch under the items on the top shelf. Add a second row of split backstitch beneath the first row. Then outline the two small vertical lines under the shelf. Repeat this process for the second and third shelves.

STEP 16: Finish. Follow the steps on page 27 to finish the hoop. Remove any transfer pen marks as needed.

16

TIP: Swap a cozy cat in place of any set of items to your bookshelves with the optional cat pattern found on page 162. For the embroidery pictured here with the pink fabric, I used 3 strands of light-gray floss to fill in the cat with split backstitch.

STITCH DIARY

"A book is a dream you hold in your hands."
—NEIL GAIMAN

Since you've picked up this book, I am sure you know the value in taking time to enjoy a simple and quiet hobby that is just for you—something like reading, baking, or crafting. I hope that with the projects and prompts in this book, you're enjoying the slow art of embroidery. So often we get wrapped up in the busyness of life and forget to take time to do the things we really enjoy! Hobbies bring us joy, connect us with friends, teach us new skills, and help break up the monotony of our workweek. What hobbies do you enjoy or want to explore more?

What do you do during your leisure time?
List some hobbies you'd like to explore to bring more
rest and relaxation to your life.

_____

_____

_____

_____

_____

_____

_____

Blush Meadow Abstract

STITCHES

- Satin stitch
- Split backstitch
- Couching stitch
- French knot
- Seed stitch
- Turkey work stitch

SUPPLIES

- 4" embroidery hoop
- 7" x 7" piece of your chosen fabric
- 1 skein of each floss color: rose gold, pale blush, ivory, metallic gold, blush
- Small gold beads
- 12" length of pale-pink bulky yarn
- 1 skein of white tapestry wool or white yarn
- Embroidery scissors
- Embroidery needle
- Beading needle
- Tapestry needle
- Transfer materials (page 20)
- Finishing materials (page 26)
- Pattern (page 163)

Your creative options are endless with this dreamy, monochrome abstract embroidery piece. Take a look through your floss, yarn, bead, and craft stash and put to use whatever feels right to you. Look for bulky yarns, shiny beads, satin floss (and more!) to give your work beautiful contrast, luster, and texture. You'll also need a pack of assorted needles for this project. A needle with a large eye, like a tapestry needle, is great for stitching with tapestry wool. A needle with a narrow eye is necessary for adding beads to your embroidery.

This project gives you an introduction to couching stitch, turkey work stitch, and adding beads, which are all oh so fun. Not feeling too adventurous? Don't worry; simply use this opportunity to practice your favorite fill stitches, like satin stitch, seed stitch, and split backstitch. The color palette I chose uses blush, rose gold, and ivory, but take a look at the inspiring examples on page 132 to see the same design stitched with different colors and stitches. Let your creative freedom take over and see what you make today! ∎

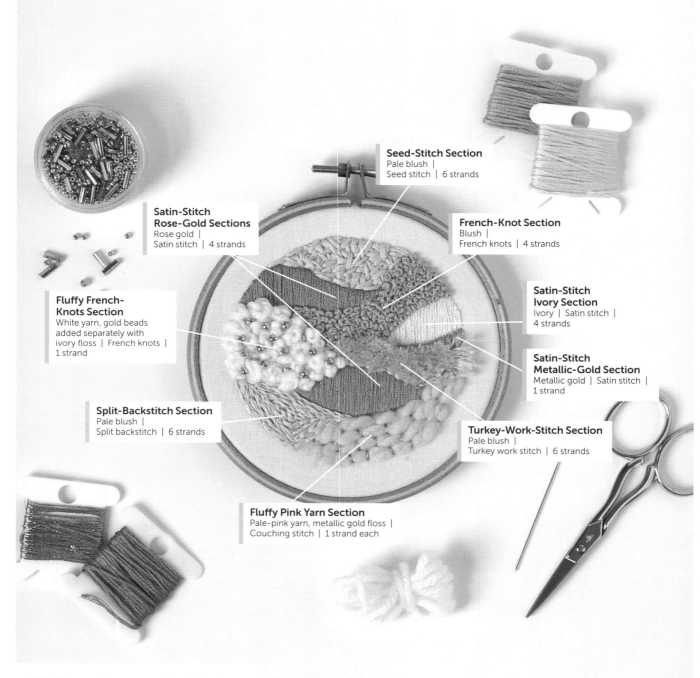

Seed-Stitch Section
Pale blush |
Seed stitch | 6 strands

**Satin-Stitch
Rose-Gold Sections**
Rose gold |
Satin stitch | 4 strands

French-Knot Section
Blush |
French knots | 4 strands

**Fluffy French-
Knots Section**
White yarn, gold beads
added separately with
ivory floss | French knots |
1 strand

**Satin-Stitch
Ivory Section**
Ivory | Satin stitch |
4 strands

**Satin-Stitch
Metallic-Gold Section**
Metallic gold | Satin stitch |
1 strand

Split-Backstitch Section
Pale blush |
Split backstitch | 6 strands

Turkey-Work-Stitch Section
Pale blush |
Turkey work stitch | 6 strands

Fluffy Pink Yarn Section
Pale-pink yarn, metallic gold floss |
Couching stitch | 1 strand each

TIP: You can jump around and stitch
any section you'd like to first, but I
recommend working on the flat sections
first, like satin stitch, split backstitch,
and seed stitch. You'll find it's much
easier to stitch these sections before
you put in French knots or turkey work.

126

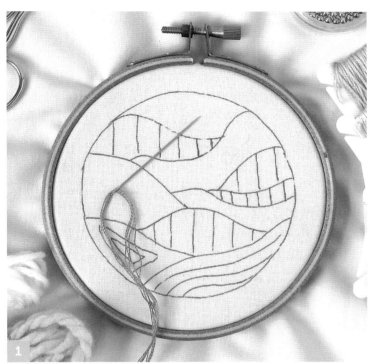

STEP 1: Prepare your materials. Following the tutorials in the Getting Started section, transfer your pattern, set your hoop, and separate your floss. Thread your needle with four strands of rose-gold floss.

STEP 2: Fill in the rose-gold satin-stitch sections. Using four strands of rose-gold floss, fill in the two sections with satin stitch. First stitch a few guidelines to help you keep your stitches parallel to one another.

STEP 3: Stitch the pale-blush split-backstitch section. Using six strands of pale-blush floss, fill in this section with split backstitch. Begin by outlining the section with a row of split backstitch, then continue adding rows of split backstitch, following the contours of the outline to the center.

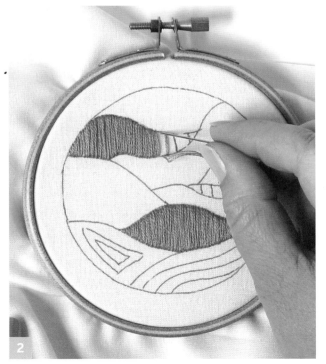

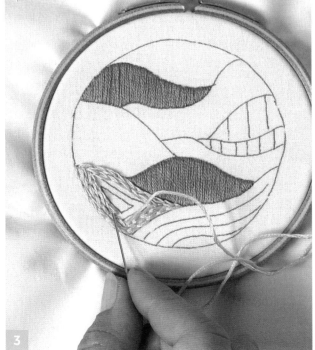

Blush Meadow Abstract

STEP 4: Fill in the ivory satin-stitch section. Using four strands of ivory floss, fill in the section in the right of the pattern with satin stitch.

STEP 5: Fill in the metallic-gold section. Using one strand of metallic-gold floss, fill in the section just below the ivory section with satin stitch. Section off parts of the shape to help you keep your stitches parallel to one another.

STEP 6: Begin the yarn-couching section. For this section, cut a 12" length of pale-pink bulky yarn and thread your needle with one strand of metallic-gold floss. Lay the yarn on top of your fabric. Bring your

needle up through the fabric and make a straight stitch across the yarn. This is a couching stitch. Pull the couching stitch taut so that the yarn is tacked into place. Repeat making couching stitches every ½" along the yarn as you guide it back and forth to fill in the section.

STEP 7: Continue the yarn-couching section. Once you have entirely filled in the section, cut the excess yarn with a pair of embroidery snips.

STEP 8: Fill in the blush French-knot section. Using four strands of blush floss, fill in this section with densely spaced French knots. Wrap the floss around

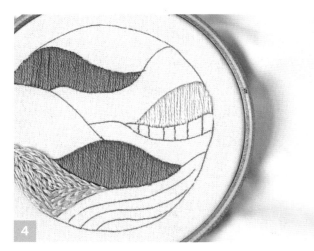

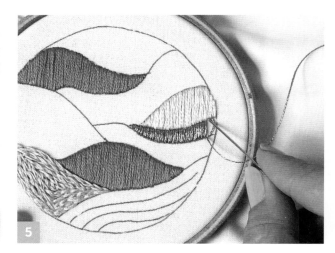

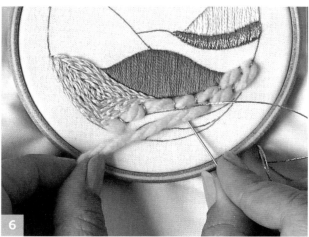

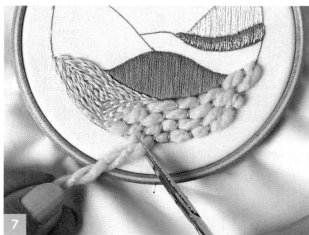

your needle once or twice, depending on the size of knot you prefer.

STEP 9: Stitch the seed-stitch section. Using six strands of pale-blush floss, fill in the top section with seed stitches. Make your stitches equal in length (about ¼" each) and place them randomly within the section. You can determine how much of your fabric shows through by how densely you place the stitches. Add multiple layers, crossing stitches over one another to cover the fabric.

STEP 10: Stitch the fluffy yarn French-knot section. Thread your tapestry needle with a 12"

length of white yarn or tapestry wool. Fill in the section with densely spaced French knots. Wrap the yarn around the needle two or three times to make the knots very full.

STEP 11: Begin adding the beads. Thread the beading or fine needle with one strand of ivory floss or any light-colored floss, knotting the tail several times. Bring the needle and floss to the front of the fabric among the yarn French knots where you want to add a bead. Pick up a bead with the needle and string it along the floss down to the fabric.

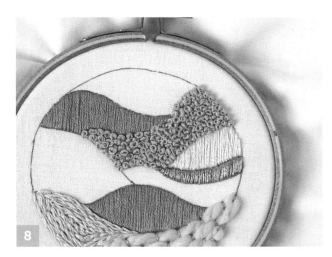

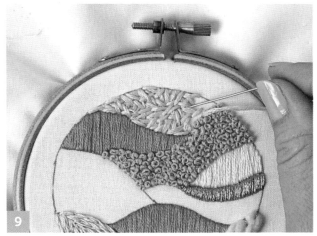

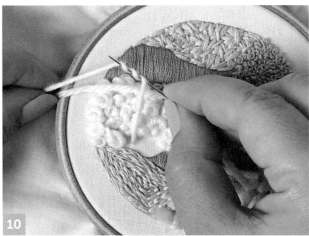

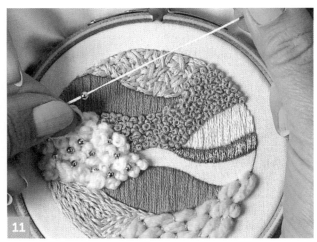

Blush Meadow Abstract

STEP 12: Continue adding the beads. Finish the stitch by pushing the needle through the fabric next to the bead, which will secure it to the top of the fabric. Continue this process to add beads throughout the fluffy French knots.

STEP 13: Begin filling in the final section with turkey work. Using six strands of pale-blush floss, fill in the final section with turkey work stitch. To make this stitch, start in the upper left corner of the shape and work in rows left to right. The closer your stitches are, the more full your pile of floss will be in the end. Start without a knot at the end of your floss and stitch down through the fabric, leaving a 1" tail of floss on top of the fabric. Bring your needle up through the fabric next to the tail and make a backstitch over it where it meets the fabric, anchoring the tail in place. Then bring your needle up right under the backstitch (or split through it) and then reenter the fabric just on the other side of the backstitch, leaving your floss in an arch on top of the fabric. Again, make a backstitch anchoring this piece of floss sticking up on the fabric. Bring your needle up right under the backstitch, and create another loop. Repeat this process, filling in the section.

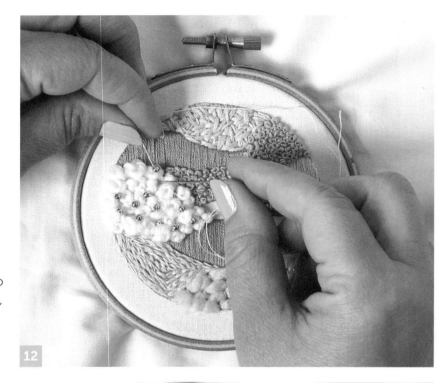

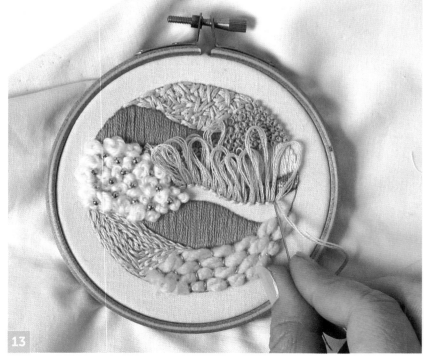

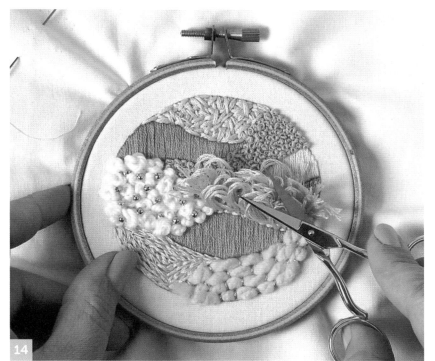

STEP 14: Finish the turkey-work section. Now that your shape is filled in with anchored loops of floss, use a pair of sharp embroidery snips to trim the loops to the length you like. Mine are about ⅓" tall. Start with a minimal cut and then go back over the area to trim more as you wish. Hint: Use a piece of clear or masking tape to remove the lint and floss scraps from your embroidery. Use your needle or a small eyebrow brush to fluff up and separate the strands to make the pile fuller.

STEP 15: Finish. Follow the steps on page 27 to finish the hoop. Remove any transfer pen marks as needed.

TIP: There are so many possibilities with this project! Look through your craft supplies collection and pull out what you're drawn to. Find chunky yarns, satiny threads, crystals, shiny beads—the list goes on. For your color palette, choose several coordinating colors, or stick to a monochromatic color scheme featuring blue, aqua, olive green, chartreuse, or other beautiful colors.

STITCH DIARY

*"Love is what carries you, for it is always there,
even in the dark, or most in the dark, but shining out at times
like gold stitches in a piece of embroidery."*
—WENDELL BERRY

This beautiful quote is worthy of being turned into a piece of embroidery,
now that you've made it this far and have fine-tuned your embroidery skills!
I hope that this book has inspired you to continue with your embroidery journey.
Embroidery is a slow craft that may not come easy at first, but if you invest your
time, patience, and practice, you can become confident in your skills as a stitcher.
Don't forget to seek help along the way and to give yourself plenty of grace as
you learn. Take a moment to think and write about your embroidery journey.

**Describe your embroidery journey. What areas do you
want to improve, and what stitches do you want to learn next?
What projects would you like to attempt?**

_____

_____

_____

_____

_____

_____

Mindful Mandala

STITCHES

- Whipped backstitch
- Reverse chain stitch
- Leaf stitch
- French knot
- Straight stitch
- Lazy daisy

SUPPLIES

- 6" embroidery hoop
- 9" x 9" piece of your chosen fabric
- 1 skein of white floss
- Embroidery scissors
- Embroidery needle
- Transfer materials (page 20)
- Finishing materials (page 26)
- Pattern (page 164)

Are you searching for a project that can help you unplug, practice mindfulness, and occupy your hands for a while? This is the one for you. I invite you to relax your shoulders, take a deep breath, get comfortable, and spend some quiet time working on filling in this mandala. Traditionally, mandalas have much purpose and spiritual meaning in many cultures around the world. Put simply, in art, mandalas are usually composed of a group of patterns that radiate from the center in a circular shape. I designed this mandala inspired by botanical shapes, which you can rearrange to stitch on pieces of clothing, accessories, or textiles outside the hoop.

While creating or coloring a mandala, and in our case stitching one with needle and thread, you can enjoy the repeating shapes and designs and perhaps even experience some of the benefits of a mandala. These pieces of ancient art are said to bring about peacefulness, improve focus, activate your creativity, and cultivate a feeling of mindfulness. Whether or not you experience those benefits from stitching this meticulous design, I know you'll at least end up with a beautiful piece of embroidery that you can display and cherish in your home. ■

Lotus Shapes
White | Whipped backstitch |
4 strands

Ivy
White | Whipped backstitch,
leaf stitch | 4 strands

Tulip Shapes
White | Reverse chain stitch,
straight stitch, French knots |
4 strands

Paisley Shapes
White | Reverse chain stitch |
4 strands

Accent French Knots
White | French knots |
4 strands

Daisy Shapes
White | Backstitch |
4 strands

Branches
White | Whipped backstitch,
backstitch, French knots |
4 strands

Dandelion Shapes
White | Backstitch, lazy daisy |
4 strands

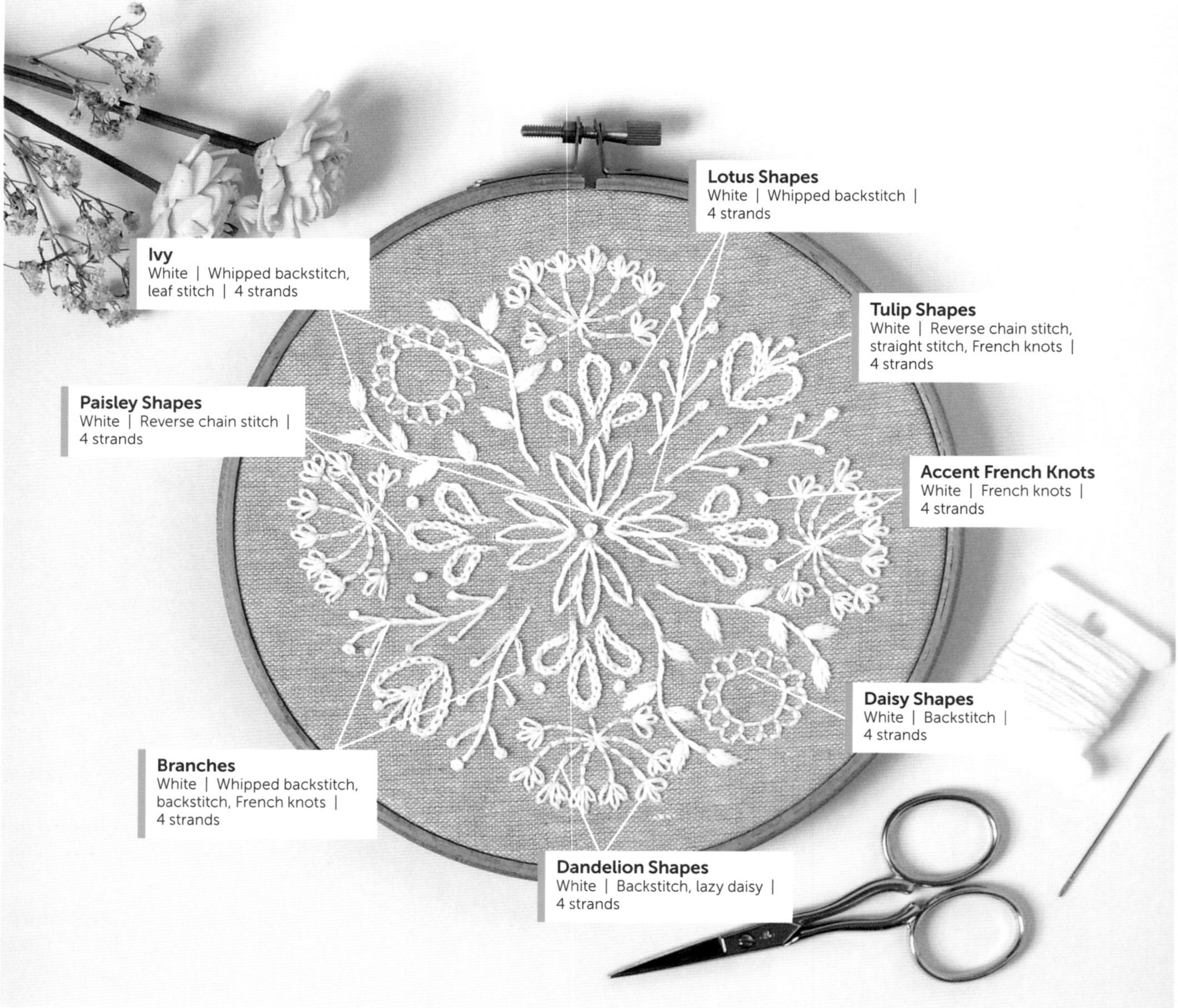

TIP: If you want to break away from
simple white, take a look through
your floss collection and choose
a floss palette that makes you feel
peace and happiness, stitching this
design in jewel tones, earth tones,
pastels, or brights.

STEP 1: Prepare your materials. Following the tutorials in the Getting Started section, transfer your pattern, set your hoop, and separate your floss. Thread your needle with four strands of white floss.

STEP 2: Stitch the center lotus shapes. Using four strands of white floss, outline the lotus flower shapes with whipped backstitch. Start by outlining the center petal, then the left and right petals, and repeat for each lotus shape.

STEP 3: Stitch the paisley shapes. Using four strands of white floss, outline the paisley shapes with reverse chain stitch.

STEP 4: Stitch the ivy. Using four strands of white floss, outline the ivy stems with whipped backstitch. Then fill in the leaves with leaf stitch.

STEP 5: Stitch the branches. Using four strands of white floss, outline the centerline of the branches with whipped backstitch. Then add the small branches with a single backstitch. Finally, add a French knot to the end of each small branch. Wrap the floss around your needle one to two times for each French knot.

STEP 6: Stitch the accent French knots. Using four strands of white floss, add a French knot wherever there is a floating dot on the pattern. Wrap the floss around your needle two to three times for each of these French knots.

STEP 7: Stitch the tulip shapes. Using four strands of white floss, outline the tulip shapes with reverse chain stitch. Then add three straight stitches to the centers of the tulip shapes. Finally, add a French knot to the end of each straight stitch.

STEP 8: Stitch the daisy shapes. Using four strands of white floss, outline the daisy shapes with backstitch. Start by stitching the circle in the middle, then outline each petal. Keep your stitches small in order to carefully follow the curved shapes of the petals.

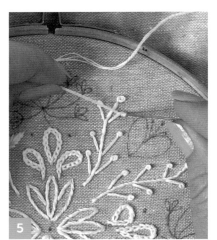

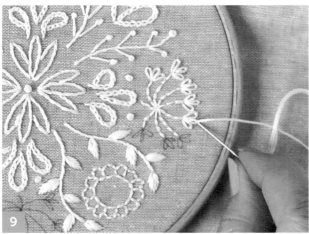

STEP 9: Stitch the dandelion shapes. Using four strands of white floss, outline the curved stems of the dandelion shapes with backstitch. Then add three tiny lazy daisy stitches to the ends of each stem.

STEP 10: Finish. Follow the steps on page 27 to finish the hoop. Remove any transfer pen marks as needed.

10

TIP: Use this design to create a daily habit centered on embroidery and mindfulness. Spend half an hour each day to stitch one piece of the design, and watch the design start to slowly unfold.

STITCH DIARY

"Smile, breathe, and go slowly."
—THICH NHAT HANH

One way to experience peace and calm within yourself is to practice mindfulness or meditation. For just a few moments each day, open your mind and tune into the present moment. Focus on one small thing and observe your sensations, thoughts, and feelings with it. A great practice to do this is to set aside some distraction-free time each day for embroidery and focus on the gentle weaving of your needle and floss through the fabric.

What are some ways that you can practice stillness, mindfulness, or meditation to bring about calm and peace in your life?

_____

_____

_____

_____

_____

_____

_____

_____

Appendix

This is your go-to reference for detailed instructions and diagrams about making the stitches in this book. Use the stitch library whenever you need a little guidance to remind yourself how to make a specific stitch. You'll also find the patterns for each project here, and a floss color index with the DMC floss color numbers I used.

Embroidery Stitch Library

Backstitch. This stitch is used for outlining. Make a straight stitch about ¼" long. Bring the needle up through the fabric about ¼" from the end of the first stitch. Stitch backward, pushing your needle through the hole at the end of the first stitch. Your stitches will be touching and sharing the same hole in the fabric.

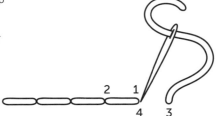

Couching Stitch. This is a stitch that simply anchors or tacks down another piece of floss or yarn that lies on the surface of your fabric. You'll want to use two threaded needles for the two lengths of floss you'll be working with. To start, use your first color of floss to create a long straight stitch on your fabric, about ½" to 1" in length (shown with A and B here). Then use your second needle and floss to create a small straight stitch across the first piece of floss, stitching up on one side of the floss and down on the other (shown with 1 and 2 here).

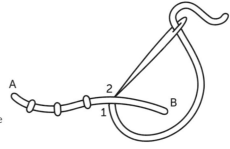

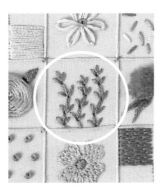

Fern Stitch. Use this stitch to outline plants, feathers, or other botanical designs. Start by making a row of backstitches for the centerline—this could be straight or curved. Then add short straight stitches where the backstitches meet. Experiment with making the straight stitches the same length or varying lengths.

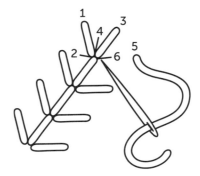

French Knot. Bring your needle up through the fabric. With one hand, hold the floss perpendicular to the fabric, gripping it tightly a few inches above the fabric. With your other hand, place your needle against the back of the floss and hold it in place while you wrap the floss around it one or two times (the more wraps, the larger the finished knot). With the looped floss on it, return your needle through the fabric, just next to the starting point. Use one hand to hold the floss out to the side, keeping it taut. As you pull the needle through the fabric, gradually and steadily release the floss. You'll be left with a tidy knot on the surface of the fabric.

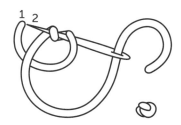

Lazy Daisy Stitch (Detached Chain Stitch). Lazy daisy stitches can be used the make petals or leaves. Start with a very tiny stitch, but do not pull the thread all the way through. Instead, let it form a loop on top of the fabric and gently hold it in place. Bring your needle up through the fabric where you want the top of the loop to be, and feed it through the loop. Pull the thread tight to bring the loop down against the fabric. Enter the fabric just above where the needle came out, capturing the top of the loop in the stitch.

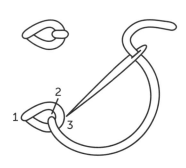

Leaf Stitch. This stitch is perfect for filling in leaves. Start with one straight stitch down the center of the leaf from the tip to about three-quarters of the way to the base. Start the second stitch by bringing the needle out on the top left side of the first stitch at the edge of the leaf. Cross over the first stitch, ending just to the right of it in the middle of the leaf. Repeat on the opposite side of the leaf. Continue stitching to the base of the leaf, keeping your stitches parallel to one another on each side.

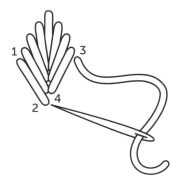

Embroidery Stitch Library, *continued*

Long and Short Stitch (Brick Stitch). Work in horizontal rows. For the first row, alternate ¼" and ⅛" straight stitches. For the following rows, use ¼" stitches. Because of the way you stitched the first row, the stitches in the subsequent rows will have alternating end points. This is a useful fill stitch.

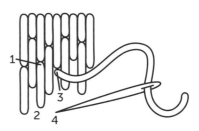

Reverse Chain Stitch. This is a stitch that can be used as a fill stitch or to create bold lines. It has the same look as chain stitch, which you may be familiar with, but what is different is the process through which it is stitched. Start by making a small straight stitch, which serves as the anchor for the chain stitch. Then come up away from the stitch about ⅕" and guide your needle under the anchor stitch, but not through the fabric. Bring the needle back down though the fabric at the last entry point, creating a chain link secured by the initial anchor stitch. Now add another chain link by bringing your needle up through the fabric one stitch length away and guiding your needle under the first chain link. Bring the needle back down through the fabric at the entry point, creating a second chain link. Repeat.

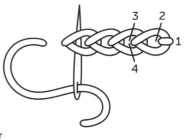

Satin Stitch. Satin stitch allows you to fill a space with smooth, flat stitches. It's especially useful for filling small shapes. Start the stitch on one side of the shape you're filling, and end it directly opposite on the other side of the shape. Repeat, making close, parallel stitches that fill the shape from one end to the other.

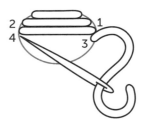

Seed Stitch. This is a fill stitch made of a group of straight stitches. The stitches are even in length but placed randomly. They can be spread out, packed in closely, and even overlapping. You can use one or more floss colors.

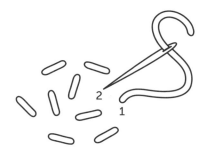

Split Backstitch. This stitch is just like backstitch, but instead of ending in the same hole as the previous stitch, you'll end in the middle of the first stitch, splitting the floss. Make a straight stitch about ¼" long. Bring the needle up through the fabric about ¼" from the end of the first stitch. Stitch backward, pushing your needle through the middle of the first stitch, splitting the floss strands in half. Because of the split, this stitch works best with either four or six strands of floss. Use this stitch for a textured outline.

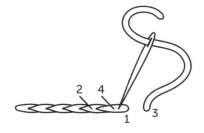

Straight Stitch (Running Stitch). This is a simple single stitch. Bring your needle through the fabric from back to front where you want the stitch to start. Then bring your needle through the fabric from front to back where you want the stitch to end. These stitches can be placed in any direction, in groups, or used alone.

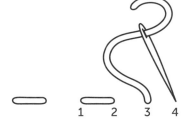

Embroidery Stitch Library, *continued*

Turkey Work Stitch. This is a stitch that creates loops, fringe, or a plush pile. To start, you won't need to knot your floss, and you'll begin on top of your fabric and stitch down, leaving a ½" tail on top of the fabric. Bring the needle up directly to the right of the tail and stitch a straight stitch across the tail, entering the fabric just to the left of the tail, anchoring the tail in place. Next, come back up under the straight stitch to the right of the tail and then stitch down about ⅛" away to the right, leaving a small amount of floss lying on top of the fabric in an arch. Make another straight stitch that anchors this loop as you did the first time. Continue creating these arches anchored by straight stitches. Fill in your shape with rows of turkey work stitch. Then use a pair of sharp scissors to trim the loops to your desired length.

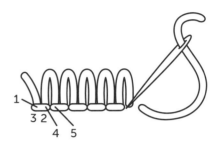

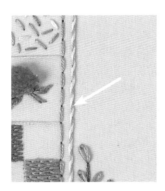

Whipped Backstitch. This is an outline stitch that makes a nice continuous line. First, stitch a row of backstitch. Then, using the same color of floss (or a different one to create a baker's twine effect), weave through the backstitches. To do this, bring your needle up through the fabric at the beginning of your row of backstitch. Guide the needle under the first stitch from right to left without entering the fabric. Repeat with the second stitch. Continue wrapping the floss around the backstitches, pulling it gently and uniformly. If the backstitches turn a corner or change direction, stitch down through the fabric to secure the floss. Then begin the wrapping process with the next section.

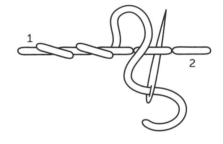

Woven Wheel Stitch. This stitch creates a 3D circular rose on top of the fabric. Start by stitching five spokes by making five straight stitches that meet in the center of your circle. Next, bring the needle up through the fabric near the center of the spokes. Guide your needle over the first spoke and under the next but do not pierce through the fabric, instead repeatedly weaving around all the spokes until the circle is filled in. Once the circle is as full as you wish and the spokes are no longer visible, stitch the needle down through the fabric.

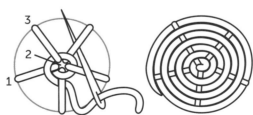

Floss Color Index

If you'd like to use the same colors that I did for these projects, here are the DMC floss color numbers so you can look for them in your local craft store. While this guide is here for your reference, you should always feel free to substitute colors or develop your own color scheme for each project!

Gentle Notes to Self
Light Mocha: 3864
Light Pine Green: 3364
Mustard: 3820

Vanilla Latte
Ivory: ECRU

Stay Awhile
Maroon: 3858
Khaki Green: 3012
White: BLANC
Light Brown: 435
Dark Gray: 645

Sweater Weather
Dark Gray: 645
Metallic Gold: G3821
Light Brown: 435
Ivory: ECRU
Mustard: 3820
Rose Gold: 3778

Let's Stay Home
Blush: 758
Light Mocha: 3864
Light Apricot: 3770
Sage Green: 523
Ivory: ECRU

Simple Countryside Bouquet
Sage Green: 523
Blush: 758
Light Tan: 437
Mocha: 3862
White: BLANC
Mustard: 3820
Light Mocha: 3864

Starry Night
Light Brown: 435
Ivory: ECRU
Metallic Gold: G3821
Mauve: 3859
Light Pine Green: 3364
Beige: 543
Soft Blue: 926
Light Gray: 648

Cozy Cottage
Ivory: ECRU
Mocha: 3862
Pale Pink: 819
Rose Gold: 3778
Khaki Green: 3012
Beige: 543
Blush: 758
Maroon: 3858

Winter Botanicals
Light Apricot: 3770
Beige: 543
White: BLANC
Dark Gray: 645
Sage Green: 523
Light Jade: 320
Mauve: 3859
Medium Blue: 931
Ivory: ECRU
Mocha: 3862
Khaki Green: 3012

Booked All Weekend
Bright Green: 470
Terra-cotta: 301
Forest Green: 520
Pale Blush: 3774
Mustard: 3820
Light Jade: 320
Blush: 758
Light Gray: 648
Sage Green: 523
Ivory: ECRU
Light Tan: 437
Light Mocha: 3864
Light Brown: 435
Brown: 632

Blush Meadow Abstract
Rose Gold: 3778
Pale Blush: 3774
Ivory: ECRU
Metallic Gold: G3821
Blush: 758

Mindful Mandala
White: BLANC

Color Theory

There is both an art and a science behind choosing your floss and fabric colors to customize a design. The art of the process is simply noticing which colors draw you in and "look nice" together. You can also apply science to color selection with some basic color theory. Have fun choosing colors for the projects, or use the Floss Color Index on page 150 to see the specific floss color numbers I chose.

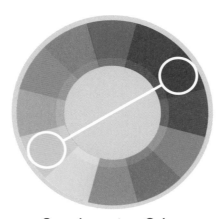

Complementary Colors
Two colors directly opposite each other
on the color wheel

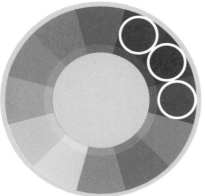

Analogous Colors
Three colors next to each other
on the color wheel

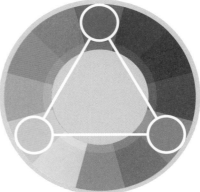

Triadic Colors
Three colors equally spaced from
one other on the color wheel

Monochromatic Colors
A collection of tints, shades, and tones of one color

Patterns

In the coming pages, you will find patterns
for all the projects in this book. I hope they
will bring you many hours of cozy stitching!
Please see page 20 for tips on how to
transfer the patterns. You can also download
all the patterns at www.betterdaybooks.com/
cozy-stitches-pattern-download.

YOU ARE ENOUGH

LET YOURSELF REST

SLOW DOWN

Gentle Notes to Self pattern, instructions on page 38

Vanilla Latte pattern, instructions on page 46

Stay Awhile pattern, instructions on page 54

Sweater Weather pattern, instructions on page 62

Let's Stay Home pattern, instructions on page 70

Simple Countryside Bouquet pattern, instructions on page 78

Starry Night pattern, instructions on page 86

Cozy Cottage pattern, instructions on page 94

Winter Botanicals pattern, instructions on page 104

Booked All Weekend pattern, instructions on page 114

Optional cat pattern

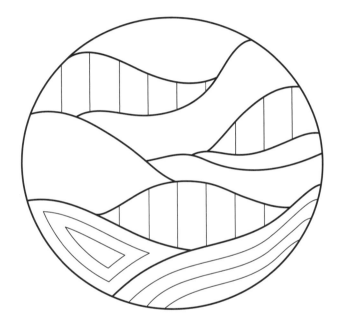

Blush Meadow Abstract pattern, instructions on page 124

Mindful Mandala pattern, instructions on page 134

Cozy Quilt sampler pattern, instructions on page 32

With *heartfelt gratitude,*
I thank you for embarking on this
cozy stitching journey with me!
I hope this book has brought you
joy and inspiration through each
project. It's my wish that the
art of embroidery will continue
to provide many moments of
tranquility and creativity
in your life.

THANK YOU
for stitching with me!

Index

Note: Page numbers in *italics* indicate projects and patterns (in parentheses). Page numbers in **bold** indicate stitch instructions.

BETTER DAY BOOKS®
HAPPY • CREATIVE • CURATED

Business is personal at Better Day Books. We were founded on the belief that all people are creative and that making things by hand is inherently good for us. It's important to us that you know how much we appreciate your support. The book you are holding in your hands was crafted with the artistic passion of the author and brought to life by a team of wildly enthusiastic creatives who believed it could inspire you. If it did, please drop us a line and let us know about it. Connect with us on Instagram, post a photo of your art, and let us know what other creative pursuits you are interested in learning about. It all matters to us. You're kind of a big deal.

it's a good day to have a better day!

www.betterdaybooks.com

better_day_books